On the Line at Subaru-Isuzu

On the Line
at Subaru-Isuzu

---

*The Japanese Model
and the American Worker*

LAURIE GRAHAM

ILR PRESS AN IMPRINT OF
Cornell University Press
ITHACA AND LONDON

Copyright © 1995 by Cornell University

Library of Congress Cataloging-in-Publication Data

Graham, Laurie, 1949–
On the line at Subaru-Isuzu : the Japanese model and the American
worker / Laurie Graham.
p.   cm.
Includes bibliographical references and index.
ISBN 0-87546-345-2. — ISBN 0-87546-346-0 (pbk.)
1. Automobile industry workers—Indiana—Lafayette.   2. Automobile
industry and trade—Indiana—Lafayette—Management.
3. Corporations, Japanese—Indiana—Lafayette—Management.   4. Fuji
Jūkogyō Kabushiki Kaisha.   5. Isuzu Jidōsha Kabushiki Kaisha.
I. Title.
HD8039.A82US58   1995
338.8'87292222—dc20   95-1253

For more information, please write to

ILR Press
Cornell University Press
Sage House
512 East State Street
Ithaca, NY 14850

*To the people who build cars and
trucks at Subaru-Isuzu*

Contents

Acknowledgments ix

1. The Japanese Model Debate 1

2. Worker Selection as a Mechanism of Control 18

3. Orientation and Training 36

4. The Work Setting 62

5. Thinking Like an Associate: Bases of Control 94

6. Working Like a Worker: Bases of Resistance 116

7. Voices from the Floor 129

Bibliography 155

Index 161

Acknowledgments

I wish to acknowledge a number of people who made valuable contributions to this book: Ruth Milkman for her suggestions for refocusing the manuscript; Randy Hodson for his enthusiastic review; Peter Seybold, Earl Wysong, and Heidi Gottfried for their insightful readings of the manuscript and constant encouragement; the people from Subaru-Isuzu Automotive who agreed to read and react to the manuscript; my major professor—Bob Perrucci—and the members of my dissertation committee—Heidi Gottfried, Harry Potter, and Nancy Gabin; faculty and graduate students at Purdue University's Department of Sociology and Anthropology for their continued support and encouragement; Bill Saxton and the "swing shift" sociology class from the Gary steel mills for helping me find the title; and finally Fran Benson and the rest of the ILR Press staff for their wonderful editorial assistance.

1

The Japanese Model Debate

The American automobile industry has become the focus of a debate concerning current changes in industrial relations. Traditionally, industrial relations in the auto industry have been organized around what has been termed a Fordist model, characterized by assembly line production methods, direct supervision, rigid job classifications, high wages, and adversarial labor relations (Milkman 1991b). Currently, a Japanese management approach, commonly referred to as "lean production" (Womack, Jones, and Roos 1990) and here called the Japanese model, represents an alternative model of labor relations. The Japanese model differs from the traditional Fordist model in that it uses workforce participation schemes, production is centered on work teams, and worker input into production improvements and quality control is emphasized.

Due to its economic success and the fact that most Japanese investment in new productive capacity is in the auto industry, the Japanese model has gained support from the U.S. government as well as industry (Howes 1992). The model is greatly influencing U.S. manufacturing, and many of its aspects are being integrated into the U.S. auto industry (Womack, Jones, and Roos 1990). Workers are being asked to accept a slowdown in wage growth, flexibility in work rules, and team-organized production in exchange for greater job security and increased union and worker participation in strategic business decisions (Katz 1985:181).

The changes that have taken place have triggered a debate concerning the effects of the Japanese model on the U.S. worker. The debate revolves around whether the Japanese model, with its team concept, is creating an era of cooperation between workers and management that is rooted in coercion or consent. Some argue that the Japanese model has ushered in a form of industrial relations that is beneficial to both workers and

1

management (Womack, Jones, and Roos 1990). Others are more skeptical and claim that the model may be beneficial to the industry but is definitely not a plus for workers (Parker and Slaughter 1988; Fucini and Fucini 1990; Berggren 1992; Dohse, Jurgens, and Malsch 1985). Critics also argue that only through union intervention can workers begin to protect themselves from speedup, work intensification, and the resulting injuries attached to the model (Robertson et al. 1993; Berggren 1992; Babson 1993).

On one side of the debate, investigators claim that the Japanese model benefits workers because it increases workers' control on the shop floor by giving them more say over the technical aspects of their work (Adler 1993a; Womack, Jones, and Roos 1990; Piore and Sabel 1984; Zwerdling 1980; Safizadeh 1991; Brown and Reich 1989). Since the 1970s researchers have suggested that modern Japanese management provides a cooperative industrial relations model based on meaningful workforce participation (Dore 1973; Cole 1979), that it emphasizes worker autonomy, that it increases differentiation of the labor force, and that it may bring an end to bureaucratic labor unions (Clarke 1990). Japanese firms experience low rates of industrial conflict, low absenteeism, low quit rates, and high productivity (Lincoln and Kalleberg 1985); this combination of factors has led to suggestions that Japanese managers have succeeded in blending technological improvements with good human relations (Hull and Azumi 1988: 427). The underlying assumption behind this body of work is that the interests of workers and management are fundamentally compatible.

A second group of theorists argues that the Japanese model has the potential to increase workers' control over work at management's expense (Derber and Schwartz 1988; Kornbluh 1984). These theorists argue that when workers get a taste of control, through participating in technical decisions, their expectations will increase and they will seek participation in other arenas. The assumption behind this perspective is that the Japanese model creates a structure that provides for meaningful worker participation in decision making.

Research grounded in the critical side of the debate challenges the positive features and conclusions cited by Japanese model supporters (Milkman 1991a; Graham 1985; Fantasia, Clawson, and Graham 1988; Dohse, Jergens, and Malsch 1985; Berggren 1992; Robertson et al. 1993; Babson 1992). The critical research argues that the participation scheme found in the Japanese model is a conscious attempt to undermine existing union organization (Slaughter 1983; Parker 1985; Parker and Slaughter

1988) and to defeat future organizational drives (Milkman 1991a; Grenier 1988). For example, a study by the International Metalworkers Federation (1992:27) for Toyota workers and their unions found that Toyota has a union avoidance strategy driving its worker selection process. Moreover, the Japanese model, with its worker participation scheme, is seen as an attempt to persuade workers to cooperate and enter into an interdependent relationship at their own expense, interdependence being woven into the very structure of production (Knights and Collinson 1985:209). It is argued that management attempts to gain workers' trust for the purpose of discouraging them from joining a union: workers are given responsibility for decision making but management nevertheless maintains tight control over the agenda offered for discussion (Tausky and Chelte 1991:336). In this way, critics argue, management hands over token control by limiting participation to very specific areas of production.

One element of the debate concerns categorization. Is the Japanese model simply a stepped-up version of Fordism or is it ushering in a post-Fordist system? The debate focuses on whether or not the model has created a kind of "factory utopia" based on a truly harmonious relationship between workers and management. My findings indicate that the debate is misfocused. As this study will demonstrate, the Japanese model is clearly post-Fordist in its approach to control over the workforce because it incorporates social elements as well as traditional Fordist methods of control. However, it does not create a factory utopia. It is grounded in Fordism but it steps well beyond Fordist principles with its focus on controlling workers' culture.

While many books deal with the Japanese system of lean production, particularly as it affects the U.S. auto industry (Fucini and Fucini 1990; Womack, Jones, and Roos 1990; Kenney and Florida 1993; Parker and Slaughter 1988), with the exception of Parker and Slaughter and the Fucinis, none addresses the debate in terms of its effects on U.S. auto workers. Fucini and Fucini are critical of the Japanese model and report on adaptation problems by Mazda workers; however, as with Parker and Slaughter, their research is limited to a unionized auto transplant. How does the Japanese model affect nonunion workers who have grown up in an economy organized around different principles? How do workers themselves view the Japanese model?

Apologists for the model such as Womack et al. (1990) declare that the Japanese model is beneficial to workers but no data are provided to support such claims (Berggren 1992; Jurgens 1993). The possibility that there may be human costs to adapting to the Japanese model—such as excessive rates of permanent injuries—is not considered. Ignoring the human factor, those theorists make claims that remain untested and perhaps untrue concerning benefits to workers. Critical researchers argue that the lean production debate is largely sustained by the "Japanese myth," charging that the description by Womack et al. of the Japanese model is pallid and often stereotyped (Jurgens 1993). The purpose of this study is to address the glaring gap in our current understanding of how the Japanese model affects U.S. workers and to offer an alternative perspective to that in the many studies uncritically calling upon U.S. industry to adopt the Japanese model.

This book contributes to the current debate by directly examining worker responses to the Japanese model. It is based on a long-term, covert, participant observation study of work experiences in a nonunion Japanese automobile transplant—Subaru-Isuzu Automotive (SIA) located near Lafayette, Indiana. This research identifies patterns of behavior that emerge among workers and between workers and management in their day-to-day experience. Such an analysis contributes numerous insights into the nature and dynamics of labor relations in a nonunion transplant under the Japanese model.

Without including the worker, the debate over the Japanese model remains somewhat speculative and superficial. To accept the conclusion that this form of organization will be beneficial to U.S. workers without supporting evidence directly from the shop floor is risky. The issue of how nonunion workers view and experience the model remains unresolved. At this point, it is unclear whether American workers benefit from the Japanese model and uncritical, generalized application of it may not meet with the expected success if the assumption that it is beneficial to workers is incorrect (Milkman 1991a:xiv).

U.S. Experiments with the Japanese Model

In order to place the Japanese model within the framework of U.S. labor relations it is important to understand the historical roots of the managerial philosophy embracing participation. In the United States the model can be seen as an extension of the job redesign movement that began during the 1970s. Job redesign occurred in response to skyrocketing absenteeism, the open sabotage of products, and wildcat strikes as illustrated by the auto workers' experiences and actions at the General

Motors plant in Lordstown, Ohio (Cole 1979). Management's approach to control at Lordstown was described as "direct order" akin to military discipline (Aronowitz 1973:33). The actions by those workers were interpreted by analysts as the reaction of an alienated workforce. One response was to "humanize" work in hopes of decreasing worker alienation and, in turn, to control absenteeism and sabotage. Humanization was to occur through job enrichment, enlargement, or redesign. It involved three principles: increasing worker participation in workplace decisions; increasing job variety; and increasing the effective use of worker potential (Cole 1979). The idea was to give meaning and purpose to individual job functions, a sense of belonging and membership in a work community, a sense of control over one's work, and opportunities for self-actualization (Blauner 1964:32–33).

Critics of the job enrichment movement maintained that the concept was of limited and short-lived effectiveness as those jobs would inevitably become routinized and boring over time (Van Maanen 1977:142) and that it did not fundamentally alter the nature of work (Braverman 1974; Edwards 1979). Others saw job enrichment as simply another management maneuver aimed at increasing control over the workforce in the historical framework of labor relations (Thompson 1989).

Quality of Work Life (QWL) programs evolved out of the job enrichment philosophy and placed worker participation at the center of the philosophical scheme. Although the actual characteristics of QWL or Quality Circles differed from one company to another, Lawler found certain aspects to be fairly universal in their application (1986:46–49): Circle members are usually volunteers from a particular work area; most have no budget; the agenda always includes a focus on improving product quality; there are usually no direct financial rewards for cost savings; most QWL programs emphasize training in group process and problem-solving techniques, have little downward sharing of information about company operations, and are not led by management but have a facilitator to help the group; Circles are typically installed in a top-down manner; and they have no formal authority except to make suggestions. Although QWL places an emphasis on participation, it is seen by critics as a political move by management to impose greater influence and control on the shop floor (Parker 1985; Grenier 1988).

In the U.S. auto industry, the National Quality of Work Life Committee began with the 1973 GM–United Automobile Workers contract and by 1983 some form of QWL could be found in over half of GM's 140 U.S. and Canadian plants (Thomas 1985:164). Ford–UAW negotiations led to an Employee Involvement (EI) program in 1979 involving 65 Ford plants (Thomas 1985:165). Chrysler has Product Quality Improvement, a program more limited in scope (Wood 1988). According to Wood (1988), the more developed worker participation programs at Ford and GM have several aspects in common. They are company-wide and viewed as an important part of corporate strategy. They are to be separate from the issues traditionally within the domain of collective bargaining. They are known as "joint" programs which are run by both union and management, using a variety of joint committees that fall within a hierarchy. And the focus is on shop floor change, most notably in the style of supervision, in cost, and in quality consciousness.

With the opening of the Honda assembly plant in Marysville, Ohio, in 1982, the Japanese model directly entered U.S. industry. In 1983 Nissan opened an assembly plant in Smyrna, Tennessee, and soon Toyota, Mazda, and Subaru-Isuzu would follow suit with independent plants or joint ventures with the Big Three auto companies (Chrysler, Ford, and General Motors).

In the 1980s GM's new plants included joint ventures, such as New United Motors Manufacturing Inc. (NUMMI) with Toyota, and Saturn, a totally new division. These new plants are based on the team concept and have no separate worker involvement programs. GM's thrust at NUMMI and Saturn is for worker participation and job redesign to be integrated through team work (Wood 1988).

Wood (1988) lists a number of ways in which these schemes have had a positive effect on work in these new, unionized auto plants. For example, the deprivation involved in a day's work is reduced (when workers are in a meeting, they are off the line). Work rules have changed to increase job rotation and responsibilities as tasks that have come with new technology have combined certain skill groups. Some deskilled jobs have been eliminated by new technology that provides ergonomic changes so that production design can be intensified without increasing work effort. Changes in decision making may have moved beyond gripes about work conditions and supervisors to examining how production is arranged. Finally, computers have aided in creating a system where workers can apply their existing knowledge to a new situation through methods such as Statistical Quality Control.

Analysts differ in their conclusions regarding technological changes and the experience of work. For example, Milkman's analysis of work in the Linden GM plant, one of the most technologically advanced auto assembly plants and GM's most efficient U.S. installation, suggests that the realities of work in the auto industry have changed little (1991b:138). She argues that the technological change led to skill polarization within the plant rather than across-the-board upgrading. Milkman states that auto production workers are experiencing more deskilling and subordination to new technology than ever before. "Their jobs, as had always been the case in the auto industry, continued to involve extremely repetitive, machine-paced, unskilled or semiskilled work. Far from being required to learn new skills, many found their jobs were simplified or further deskilled by the new technology" (Milkman 1991b:140).

Industry Analysis

In *The Machine That Changed the World,* Womack et al. reported on findings from an international survey of automobile assembly plant production. They make sweeping claims concerning the attributes of the Japanese model and how it is beneficial to its workers, stating that it continually enhances workers' skills and focuses on knowledge and experience as well as physical labor (Womack et al. 1990:55). Their claims, however, have come under much attack. For example, in his study of work organization in the Swedish auto industry, Berggren charges that Womack and colleagues make claims concerning working conditions but submit no evidence to back up their judgments: "They carefully review productivity levels, yet when it comes to conditions of work, they content themselves with cocksure assertions" (1992:4).

There has been a tendency for many analysts to emphasize the role that a worker's mental capacities play in the Japanese model. In *Beyond Mass Production: The Japanese System and Its Transfer to the U.S.,* Kenney and Florida claim that the Japanese model, referred to as Innovation-Mediated Production, represents a fundamental shift in work from an emphasis on manual to mental labor (1993:14). If their claim is true, then the model clearly signals a move away from Taylorist principles of production.

Based on my own research experiences, I believe the tendency to emphasize the role of intellectual involvement is largely due to an unquestioned acceptance of company rhetoric. After company orientation and training programs, even workers come away with similar expectations (Fucini and Fucini 1990; Graham 1993). For example, at SIA, many workers believed that a great amount of time would be spent on making decisions about work and brainstorming with teammates. An illustration of this occurred when I asked one new team member for her impression on her first day on the job. She replied: "I just didn't think it would be so physical!" Workers at SIA quickly discovered that despite their training expectations, the overriding daily experience was one of demanding, physical labor. While it is true that the model does attempt to capture workers' knowledge, when one examines the day-to-day life of working in a transplant, the overall experience of assembling a car has not changed. There has been no fundamental shift in the emphasis on physical work. While I do agree with Kenney and Florida that the model involves a fundamental shift in focus to the *social* conditions surrounding work, I believe they underestimate the continued reliance on Taylorist principles of production. It is my view that Taylorism plays a key role in the efficiency of the Japanese model and I believe my research will demonstrate that reality.

Recent research exploring the "darker corners" of the Japanese model has examined its operation and effects on workers in England, Canada, and the United States. Garrahan and Stewart's (1992) study of a Nissan plant in Sunderland, England, supports my view that company rhetoric and shop floor reality are often unrelated. They found Nissan to be an enigma in terms of its promotion of industrial change. Instead of giving workers increased control over their work, Nissan's flexibility over work assignments and its emphasis on team work and quality actually increased management's control and surveillance over the workforce. The reasons for the disparity between company rhetoric and the reality of the Japanese model as implemented at the Nissan plant are described by Garrahan and Stewart. "It is only when we carefully unpack the ideological baggage portraying the pursuit of quality as a natural and inevitable given that we perceive not only the conflict it seeks to displace (class) but also another type of conflict (individual peer competition) which it encourages" (1992:xi).

At the transplants located in North America, access by independent researchers has been limited. Only unionized companies have been open to examination by outside observers. Studies have taken place at CAMI Automotive, NUMMI, and Mazda. In some ways, this has been a curse as well as a blessing. In a union shop, workers have the privilege of criticizing their own representatives as well as the company. For example, some workers may feel the union is not moving fast enough or is moving in a direction with which they disagree. Open debate takes place, often leading to changes in policy or even in elected officials. This is how the democratic process works. A worker who feels strongly about something can get involved and work to change the situation. Workers in the unionized transplants have been very vocal at times in their disapproval of various company policies, particularly in the safety record of the transplants.

Meanwhile, the unorganized transplants have used this "worker dissatisfaction" to their advantage in fighting the union. One company message during the Nissan organizing campaign was: If working conditions are not any better with a union, why join? Of course this is a distortion. In reality, union workers are actively involving themselves in a complex process of improving their working conditions. Workers who bargain collectively with a company that has thrown out nearly every protection fought for and won decades ago are not going to change things overnight and are going to be frustrated. Over time, union workers in transplant operations are increasing their rights and protecting their interests with each round of union negotiations (see Babson 1993; Adler 1993b; Robertson et al. 1993).

Canadian auto workers have recent experience with the Japanese model. Since 1985, four transplants have located in Canada: Toyota, Honda, Hyundai, and CAMI. CAMI is a joint venture between General Motors and Suzuki and, as in the joint ventures with GM in the United States, the workers at CAMI are unionized. One of the few studies of these plants is the research of Robertson et al. (1993), a two-year longitudinal study of CAMI workers. The researchers found that the Japanese model forced the union into a position of fighting for workplace principles that had been taken for granted by the membership for years. In their survey, they found that most workers, over time, saw the concept of team spirit as meaningless. Workers said that it meant neither equality of all employees nor partnership with management. As many as seventy percent of the respondents believed that working in teams was simply a way to get them to work harder (Robertson et al. 1993:75). According to these researchers, workers regarded the CAMI principle of team spirit as an empty slogan.

U.S. Transplant Studies

NUMMI

In 1982 General Motors closed its Fremont, California, assembly plant. Two years later GM formed a joint venture with Toyota called

New United Motors Manufacturing Inc. (NUMMI) and opened the transplant in the Fremont location. NUMMI has attracted a great deal of attention not only because it was the first unionized Japanese-managed auto plant in the U.S. but also because of its high productivity and quality ratings.

When Adler (1993a) discovered that, even though the work at NUMMI is regimented and intense, NUMMI workers were more motivated and satisfied than they had been at their previous GM jobs, he set out to find out how this was possible. Historically, in plants that use strict time and motion studies as in NUMMI, worker satisfaction is low, and this is usually associated with an alienated workforce. Adler concluded that workers gain satisfaction because they are the ones designing the work procedures. Based on this conclusion, he suggests that worker involvement can humanize even the most disciplined forms of standardized work and bureaucracy: "What the NUMMI experiment shows is that hierarchy and standardization, with all their known advantages for efficiency, need not build on the logic of coercion. They can build instead on the logic of learning, a logic that motivates workers and taps their potential contribution to continuous improvement" (Adler 1993a:98). Adler calls the NUMMI experiment a "learning bureaucracy" (1993b). In an effort to improve overall quality and efficiency, the model involves workers in the design and control of their own work, increasing motivation and job satisfaction and altering the balance of power between labor and management (Adler 1993a). Adler's interpretation lends credence to the argument that the Japanese model creates a formalized system that encourages learning, captures innovation, and institutionalizes continuous improvement (1993a:98).

Turner offers an alternative interpretation for the underlying cause of worker motivation and satisfaction at NUMMI. His research suggests that the "world view" of the NUMMI workers was transformed by their experience with unemployment and plant closing and not necessarily by working under the Japanese model (1991:54). Turner describes how the laid-off workers returned to the plant in a "grateful" frame of mind for the week of unpaid screening and testing required to apply for work at NUMMI (1991:57). A type of economic discipline had been applied to those workers. Turner reports that despite worker participation in decisions at NUMMI, management retains the ultimate say regarding work standards (the number of tasks each worker performs), equipment use, sourcing decisions, and product and other strategic planning (1991:59). What has changed from the traditional system is that the union gets a steady flow of information and is brought in on early discussions regarding the above issues (Turner 1991).

Further insight into the nature of work under the Japanese model can be gained by comparing Adler's findings at NUMMI to Kamata's (1982) experience at Toyota in Japan. Kamata worked as a temporary employee in a Toyota factory. He found the Japanese model to be a system of intense management domination. Kamata notes that the company made constant demands for unscheduled overtime and speedup. Workers were forced to work many hours beyond the normal work day in order to reach production quotas. If workers were absent, either the team leader or another line worker had to do the additional job (Kamata 1982).

Lending support to Kamata's experience, Dohse, Jurgens, and Malsch (1985) characterize the Japanese model (Toyotism) as the practice of Fordism where management prerogatives are largely unlimited. A concrete example is how continuous improvement is achieved. A regular procedure is to pull workers deliberately off the line when it is running smoothly in order to force the remaining workers to speed up (Dohse et al. 1985:131). Dohse and his co-workers argue that this type of flexibility means that individual workloads are in principle always open to increase and intensification (1985:132).

In defense of the model, Adler suggests that Kamata may be biased in focusing on Toyota's temporary workers; NUMMI has no temporary workers. Additionally, Adler believes that the extreme exploitation Kamata describes would be difficult to transfer to other industrialized countries. However, I found that workers at SIA experienced many of the difficulties that Kamata describes, such as unannounced overtime, speedup, and exploitation of temporary workers.

Brown and Reich point to two significant factors for NUMMI's success. First, they argue that pre-employment screening played a pivotal role in shaping NUMMI's cooperative workforce in two ways: Workers who knew they would not fit in with the new style of management were unlikely to put themselves through the extensive screening process, and the screening process was an integral part of attitude transformation (Brown and Reich 1989:31). Secondly, they point out that NUMMI started with an entirely new management team with a different philosophy. Therefore, the direct, personal distrust that had developed between worker and manager was eliminated.

Mazda

Mazda Motor Manufacturing (USA) Corporation is located in Flat Rock, Michigan, thirty miles south of Detroit. As at NUMMI, the Mazda workers are represented by the United Auto Workers union. Ford owns twenty-five percent of the Japanese parent company. Although NUMMI was forced by union pressure to hire mainly from the pool of workers laid off from GM's Fremont plant, Mazda had freedom to hire anyone (Parker and Slaughter 1988:178).

During their three-year study of Mazda, Fucini and Fucini (1990) found that initially, workers had high hopes for the Japanese model. When the plant reached full production, however, those same workers found the reality of working in the plant to be quite different from the early promises of team spirit.

More recently, Babson conducted a survey of all twenty-four hundred workers at Mazda. He found that workers experienced the Japanese model not only as lean but also as mean. Asked if they could sustain their present work intensity, three out of four workers said they would be injured or worn out before they reached retirement (Babson 1992:16). At the same time, however, Babson found that workers were in the process of changing the system through the union. He describes several ways in which workers are challenging the Japanese model's potential for unilateral management control. For example, workers won changes in the role of the team leader. Team leaders are now elected and subject to recall by team members, and team leaders will no longer take attendance, offer overtime, or distribute paychecks. Babson claims that workers are attempting to change the team leader from a "junior foreman" to a leader, trainer, and relief worker (1992:26). In addition to changes in the team leader's role, the company's widespread use of temporary employees has been eliminated and replaced by an agreement that temporary employees can only be used if there is mutual agreement between the union and the company concerning their use and number. Moreover, temporary workers will not be used to avoid hiring regular full-time employees (Berggren, Bjorkman, and Hollander 1991:28). The union has also won parity with Big Three wages.

The conflicting analyses of NUMMI and Mazda illustrate the lively debate taking place over the nature and effects of the Japanese model. NUMMI and Mazda are interesting cases because for the first time, an independent, industrial union is confronting various features of the Japanese model. The balance of power that is created when workers organize should not be underestimated. As Milkman stressed in her study of Japanese plants in California, fear of unionism is what shapes management's behavior: "My interviews with both union organizers and managers suggest that the determination of these firms to combat unionism cannot be emphasized too strongly" (1991a:111).

Saturn

In 1990 the first car came off the assembly line at General Motors' Saturn assembly plant—a plant created to mimic the Japanese model of production. Saturn is located in Spring Hill, Tennessee, a greenfield site far from Detroit. However, unlike the greenfield locations of Japanese transplants (Perrucci 1994), GM did not locate in Tennessee in order to operate a nonunion plant. All workers at Saturn came from other GM locations and are seasoned UAW members. No workers were recruited locally. Saturn is a noteworthy case because the UAW's response to the Japanese model has evolved to its greatest extent through the Saturn workforce.

In their analysis of the Saturn assembly plant, Rubinstein, Bennett, and Kochan (1993) describe experiences that go far beyond the worker participation scheme found in the Japanese model. They refer to the UAW's negotiated "partnership structure" of governance as having created a potential conduit for real gains in worker autonomy. The partnership structure attempts to protect and promote workers' interests at nearly every level of decision making. As a safeguard, the union has created a system of democratic checks to prevent each participant's self-interest from overshadowing the interests of the general workforce so that union participation will not be coopted and unresponsive to rank-and-file concerns (Rubinstein et al. 1993:360).

The SIA Study: Background and Methods

The present research focuses on my work experience within a nonunion Japanese automobile transplant. From July 1989 through January 1990, I worked as a covert participant observer at Subaru-Isuzu Automotive (SIA). Both management and workers were unaware that they were under observation.

On February 2, 1989, I completed an application for production work at SIA. The application was the first step in the company's pre-employment screening process, a process that I was involved in over the next six months. That July I was hired, and after undergoing the company's orientation and training program, I began working in the plant three weeks later. I was assigned to Team 1 in the Trim and Final department and worked with my teammates for six months until I left employment on January 12, 1990.

This was not my first factory job. That had been in the 1970s in Waterloo, Iowa, where I worked at a plant assembling hog houses to be trucked to farms. The company, Farmstead Industries, hired another woman and me at the same time. Her boyfriend was a white-collar worker there and had inside information that the company was planning to hire two women. She approached me, and we applied that day. As we walked to work the following day, I remember discussing the responsibilities that we carried on our shoulders. We believed that if we were unsuccessful, it would not only be a personal failure; in that era when women were beginning to break into traditionally male jobs, we felt that women were depending on our ability to stick it out. I held a variety of jobs at that factory. I worked on a team that built floors, back walls, and roofs. Later, I built ventilation chambers and finally I became the "electrician" doing the wiring on the buildings. All the work was physically demanding.

When we began working at the hog house plant it was unorganized. However, within a few months I was approached by two other workers and asked to be part of the organizing committee. The three of us signed up over two-thirds of the workforce within a few weeks, an election was held, and workers voted overwhelmingly for union representation with the International Association of Machinists and Aerospace Workers. During my years at that factory, I was elected to the negotiating committee and was shop steward. Although I had no previous union experience and I could not have described what a union was before working at that plant, I became a staunch union advocate.

Since then, I have held only one job before SIA that actually included assembly line work. One summer I worked in a parts packaging plant where I stood in front of a belt-type assembly line with several other workers. Each of us would insert a particular part into a container as it passed in front of us. This was a nonunion plant that specialized in employing students from the local university at five dollars an hour. We worked six-hour shifts with one ten-minute break. During that summer, there was no talk of unions. People considered these good temporary jobs as the company was willing to work around student schedules. The assembly line work was not physically demanding but it was incredibly boring.

I have also been a cook, waitress, service worker, and union organizer before becoming an assistant professor. All those years of blue-collar work did not prepare me for working on an automobile assembly line, however. The line was both physically demanding and emotionally draining. While employed at SIA, I would often dream about the line. Sometimes I would wake up and find myself thinking about my work station. I began waking up long before my alarm sounded at 4:45 A.M., afraid of being late for work. (I was not the only worker to experience this type of anxiety; several of my team members discussed various sleep disturbance experiences.)

Because I was not a novice to the rigors of factory life, I did not appear to be an outsider at SIA—a possible drawback in participant observation (Whyte 1984). This and the fact that many of my SIA co-workers had some higher education meant there were few real cultural barriers to overcome.

My analysis is drawn from informal discussions with 46 female and 104 male co-workers (including 6 male managers and 4 Japanese trainers) throughout the plant, from day-to-day participant observation of co-worker and worker-management interactions, and from documents distributed by the company.

A possible limitation of the study concerns the time period. It is unique in that my research occurred during the company's initial months of production. Since that time, my sources in the plant report that many changes have occurred. Workers today experience a faster assembly line, a second shift now exists, and temporary workers work side by side with regular employees. However, a unique aspect of the start-up period is that it is particularly conducive for understanding the emergence of work culture and shop floor relations. A certain amount of excitement over beginning production existed among many workers, providing an ideal setting for management to take advantage of workers' optimism to induce a spirit of cooperation and pulling together to beat the competition. Therefore, patterns that emerge contrary to this goal serve as evidence of management's inability to transfer a message of cooperation, team spirit, and worker empowerment through the Japanese model.

A definite advantage of working during plant start-up was that it often allowed me free access to other departments and areas within the plant. During start-up, there were problems getting the Paint department up and running on a continuous basis. On several occasions, our line would be down for an entire day or at least for several hours. When this occurred, I would find excuses to leave my area and investigate other sections of the plant. This was fortuitous, enabling me to question workers from other departments and areas informally and to observe them at work. By contrast, when Chinoy worked on an assembly line as a participant observer in an auto plant, he found himself so tied to the line that it was difficult to talk to other workers (Chinoy 1955).

Acting as a participant as well as an observer involves the researcher in an active role in the research setting and assumes that the researcher's experiences will be similar to those of other workers. I entered the study fully aware that one of the difficulties of this methodology is maintaining a balance between depth of involvement as an insider and retaining the distance needed to observe from the outside.

Gaining employment and working in the plant as a hidden participant observer was the method of choice not only because entry could not otherwise be gained with management's knowledge but for several additional reasons. Entering a plant without the knowledge of management or workers speeds up the process of gaining acceptance from co-workers and management (Hodson and Sullivan 1990). It is also least disruptive to the natural course of events—people may attempt to modify their behavior if they know they are under observation. Another advantage of this type of methodology is that it allows for questions to be asked and observations to be made as events occur (Bollens and Marshall 1973). It provides a means to identify categories of behavior as they emerge in their natural contexts. This methodology also enables the researcher to observe patterns of opposition embedded in what are often mundane interactions (Gottfried and Sotirin 1991). Finally, participant observation is well suited for a study of the shop floor and has been the method of choice by other researchers when attempting to understand shop floor culture and experience (Pfeffer 1979; Linhart 1981; Kamata 1982; Cavendish 1982; Molstad 1988). However, participant observation occurs within situations as they are found, which may not facilitate social interaction: the atomization and fragmentation characteristic of many labor processes keep workers tied to their tasks, precluding the participant observer from much social intercourse (Knights and Collinson 1985:205). As indicated, conducting this research during plant start-up helped somewhat but in addition, to overcome this problem and to compare my workplace experiences with those of others, the study combines interviewing with participant observation techniques.

In the course of developing this project, one practical concern regarding my methodology and my ability to assess the factory environment while also functioning as a regular worker involved how I would be able to collect notes while working on the line. Luckily, the station that I worked during my last few months required that I carry a clipboard for noting damage to the car bodies as they entered our area; hence it was not unusual to see me jotting down notes. However, even before I was assigned to that particular station, I was able to stand next to one of my parts racks and take down notes. Each team member had paper and pencil for noting parts shortages and for keeping daily records on car numbers and various other assigned duties. It was not out of the ordinary to observe people writing. My normal routine was to have small scraps of paper and a pen in my pocket. I would jot down a few notes while working and stuff them in a pocket. During lunch and sometimes on breaks I would expand on my notes in the bathroom. Every day, after work, I sat down at my computer and entered the day's report from my notes. Some days there would be little to report. Most of the time, however, there was much to record. A factory is a politically charged environment of vigorous social dynamics.

2

Worker Selection as a Mechanism of Control

A critical component in the Japanese model is pre-employment screening. In their study of seven Japanese auto transplants in the United States, Berggren, Bjorkman, and Hollander (1991) found employee selection to be a key factor in those transplants' high productivity. The fact that the hiring process at transplants tends to differ sharply from the traditional approach used by the U.S. auto industry is well documented. In the United States, recruitment has traditionally consisted of matching the most qualified individuals with the desired skills for a specific job category (Marx 1988). This is typically accomplished by documenting an applicant's past experience through labor bureau records (Klug 1989). On the other hand, Japanese recruitment seeks to find the individual with the "proper character whom it can train" (Marx 1988: 280). Instead of searching for applicants with necessary skills for the job, the focus is on social background, temperament, and character references (Woronoff 1981; Boisot 1983).

At Mazda, Hill, Indegaard, and Fujita found that interpersonal skills were more important for landing a job than were physical dexterity and past work experience (1989:74). Toyota's recruitment process is reported to be similar and relies on two premises: the "cognitive appropriateness" of prospective employees; and that "appropriate psychological characteristics" are identifiable and can be harnessed for the requirements of the company (Garrahan and Stewart 1992). Workers at Subaru-Isuzu Automotive also found that the criterion for selection was based on their interpersonal performance during the selection process and not on any particular technical skill or experience they might possess.

In most blue collar jobs, the traditional American pattern of hiring and employment is based on an unspoken agreement between workers and management. Workers enter into the employment relation intending to perform the job to the best of their ability. In return, workers expect their individuality to be respected and their values and beliefs not to be scrutinized or questioned. One goes to work and does the job and management does the same. There is no extensive hiring process; workers and management typically enter into the relationship as relative unknowns.

At SIA, I found that the intensive pre-employment screening process potentially broadens the traditional arena of adversarial labor relations by bringing a formal system of control into play long before a worker even lands a job. Pre-employment screening functions as a gatekeeper and, by targeting a worker's attitude and value system, it may create a new level of management control on the shop floor. While a more traditional approach to management focuses on controlling the technical aspects of work, the Japanese model focuses on the social aspects of work and the relationships formed while work is being done. Advanced technology provides the machinery for intensifying production, and the Japanese model aims to create a workforce willing to keep up with those machines. The goal is to maintain even higher levels of productivity.

Even though pre-employment screening is a necessary component in the overall success of the Japanese model, at SIA it created unanticipated consequences in the behavior of job applicants. Many applicants sensed a contradiction between the company's egalitarian, team philosophy and its highly competitive hiring process. They responded by manipulating the system, their manipulative behavior taking the form of a charade. Successful applicants reported lying on questionnaires and pretending to be team oriented in order to get through the selection process.

From February 1 until July 10, 1989, I collected several types of data at various points in time as a hidden participant observer in the pre-employment selection process. First, during selection, I relied on direct observation and informal conversations with employment specialists and job applicants. Second, at the end of each day I sought out applicants' reactions to that phase of the process. Finally, throughout my six months in the plant, I continued to gather data through informal conversations with regular workers and with newly hired team members as they recollected their selection experiences.

Following is a detailed description of the hiring process. Next is an analysis of worker response to the process and an assessment of its net impact on workers. The final section of this chapter discusses the theoretical implications of this type of employment screening.

The Selection Process

To gain employment at SIA, prospective full-time production workers submit to a battery of tests and observed exercises administered by the Indiana Department of Employment and Training (DET). The offices for handling SIA hiring are several miles from the regular DET office. Prospective applicants fill out two forms, one a standard two-page application for registering with the DET and the other a ten-year work history including dates of employment, job titles and duties, hourly rates of pay, days missed per year, and the applicant's reason for leaving each job. During selection we were told that thirty thousand people had applied to work at SIA. When the forms are completed, each applicant is scheduled to take the General Aptitude Test (GAT). The DET provides the initial screening. SIA does not enter into the process until the final step, an interview at the plant.

During my initial visit to the special DET office, I picked up a booklet titled *Subaru–Isuzu Automotive, Inc.: Facts and Information,* available to all applicants. Although consisting of only five pages, it contained enough information to give a clear idea of the company's philosophy and what it was searching for in its applicants. The booklet offered a general description of the size of the facility, indicated the number of cars and trucks expected to be built per year, and said the company would use state-of-the-art manufacturing techniques with a blend of Japanese and American management practices.

SIA was looking for people with "a high work ethic," said the booklet. Included were five questions to ask oneself before applying to SIA: "Am I committed to the concept of 'Quality Consciousness?' Am I willing to share my ideas with others and to constantly strive to improve in all areas? Am I ready to work in a fast-pace work environment? Can I work with others in a team? Does SIA sound right for me?" The importance of the team and cooperation are stressed: "SIA is not hiring workers. It is hiring associates . . . who work as a team to accomplish a task. . . . cooperation among associates is very important." The booklet compares team leaders to basketball team captains and group leaders to coaches. It describes how trust and "kaizen" are important concepts at SIA. Associates would be trusted with the responsibility "for quality and production-line safety" and were expected to kaizen, that is, "to search for a better way to do a job more easily, more efficiently, or more safely."

The message is clear. SIA is searching for team players, people who are cooperative and willing to strive toward greater efficiency.

Eight of the twelve scheduled applicants, three women and five men, appeared to take the GAT test, consisting of nine written and four dexterity tests. The written tests included word association, word comprehension, simple mathematics, story problems, and spatial comprehension. One dexterity test involved placing tiny plastic pegs into closely spaced holes. A second test involved disassembling and reassembling tiny brass washers and pegs. Scores were based on the number of tasks performed accurately within a specified time. After the dexterity tests, I was made acutely aware that I had the lowest score, as we were instructed to call out the number of pegs we had completed at the end of each test.

Applicants receive the GAT results by mail. According to the letter I received, the test was assessed by creating universal clusters of five top groups referred to as families. Each applicant's test score was then converted to a percentile ranking comparing his or her score to those of employed workers in that cluster. The higher the ranking, the greater one's aptitude for a particular family of jobs. For production workers, SIA was focusing on Job Family IV. For that family of jobs, seventy-three percent of the score was compiled from the tests on learning ability, verbal aptitude, and numerical aptitude. Twenty-seven percent was from the psychomotor component: motor coordination, finger dexterity, and manual dexterity. I telephoned the DET office and a worker assured me that, since I ranked in the eighty-ninth percentile in Job Family IV, I should receive a letter within three weeks scheduling me for a Phase I assessment.

During the period between receiving my GAT score and participating in Phase I, I experienced several frustrating moments with the hiring system. My application was "lost in the computer" on two separate occasions and if I had not persevered, I would simply never have heard from those in charge of hiring. At the end of each phone call to the DET, I was told that I would be receiving a letter from them very soon. When a week had gone by with no letter, I would call again. Finally, during my third phone conversation with the employment representative, I said: "Look, I'm thirty-nine years old. Don't you hire women over thirty-five?" At this point, she assured me, once again, that it was all a mistake and that they did not discriminate in hiring by age or any other factor. They told me I would be scheduled for Phase I in the immediate future and I was.

On April 22 I received a letter congratulating me on having been "selected to enter Phase I of a two phase pre-employment assessment activity" and I was scheduled to participate on May 9. However, I had a scheduling conflict. I informed the DET office; they readily accommodated me. I was rescheduled two weeks earlier on April 25. Due to the rescheduling, I was tested with a group of welders as DET would not be testing general production workers for at least another week.

Phase I began promptly at 8:00 A.M. and continued for four hours. As each person signed in, we were asked to present some form of picture identification. Applicants were directed to a large room with tables arranged in a U. Although the room was set for twenty participants, only sixteen were present. I was the only female and the other applicants included one African American and one Hispanic man.

Before the testing began, the coordinator of the screening process gave the applicants an opportunity to ask questions about SIA. In response to a question concerning job prospects, the coordinator said that SIA was hiring a total of forty-five welders. When asked about production work he responded: "If any of you men are not chosen as welders [they were all aware that I was not a welder], you could still be considered for production work providing that you scored eighty percent or better on Job Family IV of the GAT test." In response to a question regarding when we would find out the results of Phase I, he told us that each of us would receive a letter by the middle of the following week informing us whether or not we had been selected to continue to phase II. Asked what our chances were, he replied: "Only forty-six percent of Phase I applicants make it to Phase II. However, most of those are eventually hired."

One piece of information the coordinator volunteered suggested that a union was unnecessary and possibly detrimental: "Benefits at SIA are comparable to any UAW shop and better than some, especially after the concessions they have been giving." I found that, for the most part, applicants were unaware of any of the specific benefits that the UAW had won at the Big Three plants. The coordinator was careful to not specify just which SIA benefits were "better" than the UAW's. (After I was hired, I discovered that none of the benefits were superior or even equal to those in most UAW auto shops and the wages were certainly lower.)

The first test in Phase I was an attitude questionnaire consisting of 120 statements. We were to react to each statement by checking one of five choices ranging from strongly disagree to strongly agree. The questions seemed to cluster into a few common areas: Willingness to work with other people, concern over product quality, interest in solving problems as a group, attitude toward supervisors, and desire to learn new jobs and skills. There was one subset of questions to which we were to respond as though we were maintenance workers and another calling for response as if we were team leaders.

In most instances, the answers that matched the qualities the company was seeking in employees seemed fairly obvious (and this was later confirmed by other applicants). For example, when responding to the statement: "Problems can be solved between employees and management through talking," I felt that the "correct" answer was pretty straightforward. My only dilemma was just how strongly I should agree.

After completing the questionnaire, we were separated into teams of four. The teams were led to separate rooms where we engaged in decision-making and problem-solving exercises. All applicants wore name tags and had name plates on the table in front of them so that the observers could be certain to attribute each statement to the correct applicant. We were informed that everything we said would be written down by the observers. Our comments would then be assigned a numerical ranking. We were told that we must score at a certain level in order to pass Phase I and be able to continue to the next phase in the selection process.

My team's first exercise involved three observers. We were to build a series of circuit boards. The overall task was to be completed in one hour. The hour was divided into segments of approximately fifteen minutes in which only certain aspects of the exercise could take place. Team members were to decide, as a group, which circuit to build and then how to approach the assembly. We were given money to buy parts from one of the observers. Then we were to assemble a circuit and have it inspected. If it passed inspection, it was to be sold to the observer. Our mission was to sell enough assembled circuit boards to make a profit. Our decisions and planning were to be completed within the first fifteen-minute period. During the second period, we were to buy all of the parts, complete the assembly, have the circuits inspected, and collect our money. The two timed periods would then be repeated.

Our first attempt seemed to end in utter failure—we had purchased enough parts to build four circuits and had barely finished one! Our strategy was to build one of the more complicated circuits. We thought that since the return on our investment would be greater, we would be able to build fewer circuits. We soon discovered that the exercise was much more difficult than we had anticipated. Getting the boards to pass inspection was nearly impossible. Everything had to be absolutely perfect. On the second round the team changed its strategy and we focused on an easier circuit, hoping to make up for our error through volume.

The atmosphere in the room during the circuit board exercise was very tense. Each of us knew that whether or not we were successful in landing a job depended on our every word and action. Such intensity quickly separated out those of us who were able to function effectively under pressure. For example, I observed two teammates as they worked furiously toward the stated goal of the exercise. They narrowly focused all of their attention on production in an effort to make a profit. Because they were working so hard, they were saying very little so there would be no information on which to base a score. To fight this tendency, I tried to keep in mind that it was our interactions that the observers were scoring and not the number of circuit boards the team would actually assemble.

My overall strategy going into the selection process was to take on the qualities of a team player. Taking this approach, I threw myself into the role of supporter. I encouraged others, offered a few suggestions, and gave my full cooperation when any team member came up with what seemed a reasonable suggestion. It was apparent during the task that the aforementioned two highly focused team members did not understand the underlying criteria for selection. By throwing themselves into the task of assembling the boards, they limited their communication with other team members. By working so diligently, they were quite likely eliminating themselves from the competition. Phase I was, clearly, a means for assessing social behavior in terms of willingness and ability to cooperate with others, not one's ability to produce.

Shortly after the first exercise I discovered that I was not alone in this assessment. After the first task, all of the teams returned to the general meeting room. For a few minutes applicants were without the presence of observers, so we exchanged impressions. When discussing the circuit board exercise, an applicant from another team said: "It doesn't matter if your team makes a big profit; in fact, you aren't even supposed to make much of one. That's why it's so difficult. A friend of mine, who got hired on at SIA, clued me in to what is going on."

The second team scenario was another problem-solving task. Once again, we were to make our decisions as a team. We were to decide on the best way to handle a complex scheduling problem. The scenario involved an auto shop that employed several mechanics with a wide variety of skills, certifications, and technical expertise. We were able to schedule each mechanic into an appropriate job. Of course, there were more jobs than people, and certain tasks were given priority over others, but even with the added difficulties, it was a much easier task than the first exercise. The team finished early.

While waiting for the other teams to finish, we visited with our observer. One team member told us that he was originally from the Lafayette area and had seen military service in Korea and Vietnam. "After twenty-six years in the army, I retired as soon as I heard about this plant opening up. My experience in the service gives me the kind of preparation that is needed to work in a plant like SIA," he said. Based on his performance during the first task, I was not optimistic about his chances. He was one of the two who had worked diligently at assembling his circuit instead of interacting with the team. Perhaps that was the reason for his outburst. After the applicant from the other team had revealed what he believed to be the underlying intent of the exercise, the veteran may have realized his error and hoped to impress the observer and make up for his poor showing during the first exercise.

At the end of Phase I, several of us gathered in the parking lot to discuss our experiences. One applicant said he was "wiped out"; another expressed "surprise at the intensity of the day." In the parking lot, the applicants who had not been on the same team tended to interact with each other instead of with their teammates. This might have been due to the intense competition that surfaced within teams. For example, one applicant complained, "One guy on my team just wouldn't shut up and the rest of us couldn't get a word in edgewise." Even though many applicants expressed concern that they might have been overshadowed, at the same time they acknowledged that we had all shared a unique experience. We wished each other luck and went our separate ways.

The following week, I received a letter congratulating me for having been selected to enter Phase II of the selection process. I was scheduled for Phase II on May 5. Once again, I had a scheduling conflict and the DET office accommodated me by rescheduling me on June 5. The letter said Phase II would be an all-day assessment. We were to bring our lunches as no one would be allowed to leave the building.

All ten applicants that were scheduled to participate in Phase II were present. Everyone was from either the local community or the surrounding area. There were eight men and two women. Everyone was white. I recognized no one from Phase I.

Generally, Phase II tested individual performance under stressful conditions. We were given timed assembly tasks and individual problem-solving exercises. Applicants were divided into two groups of five and led to separate rooms. Our group entered a room with five large plywood boards. The observer called the exercise "The Manufacturing Task." Each board measured eight feet by twelve feet and had nine tire rims bolted to it in three diagonal rows. Our assignment was to remove and replace a minimum number of rims within a specified time, by following detailed written instructions. Each applicant was given a tire iron to remove and replace color-coded lug nuts, and steel toe covers to strap to his or her shoes. Then we chose our boards. While we worked, the observer checked our progress and inspected the tension on the lug nuts.

The steel "toes" were awkward and noisy, but so was every other part of the task. Tire irons rang as they were dropped on the floor, lug nuts dinged as they rolled across the room, and steel toes clanked with every step. We were given one hour to complete the manufacturing task. We were told that we had to average one minute and forty seconds per rim for a total of forty rims in order to pass the exercise. The observer assured us that it should not be difficult to achieve as "even a pregnant woman had managed to meet the quota." At the end of the hour, we were bathed in sweat. There were complaints of aching backs from bending over and of bruised arms from the twirling tire iron. In addition to being physically demanding, the exercise imposed the added pressure of making quota, which tested one's self-control and determination as much as one's skill or speed.

After I was hired, nearly everyone in my orientation class (I began at SIA with forty other workers in an orientation class) commiserated over the tire rim task. Tall people complained about having had to bend over to work on the bottom row of rims. Short workers complained that the top row had been above their heads, which made it particularly difficult to spin the tire iron without hitting one's arm. The physical demands of the tire rim task left a big impression on all of us. No one in the class wanted to be assigned that job in the plant.

The second task of Phase II involved assembling a series of fuel filters and rubber hoses. We were directed to follow a specific routine when retrieving parts for each individual filter and to follow specified procedures during the actual assembly. The room was arranged so that we bumped into each other when picking up parts and, to add to our frustration, we were assigned to tables that were several inches lower than a comfortable working height. When an applicant finally managed to assemble a filter, it was carefully inspected and, often, rejected. Every screw and clamp had to be perfectly positioned with just the right amount of tension. Once again, we were cautioned that in order to pass Phase II, we had to make quota.

At the end of both the first and second exercises we were given twenty minutes to write down our individual suggestions for improving productivity. After the second suggestion period, we broke for lunch. During lunch, several applicants complained that Phase II was not what they had expected; they had not expected it to be so physically demanding.

There was only one team-centered activity in Phase II, a problem-solving exercise. In thirty minutes each team was to decide, by consensus, on the three most advantageous improvements for the tire rim operation. We were told that the improvements were to address the operating procedure, equipment, parts, or the physical aspect of the work. While our team discussed its options, two observers recorded our conversations. One team member volunteered to write down our ideas and we proceeded.

Compared to my team members in Phase I, Phase II team members were much more aggressive. They were more verbal, came up with more ideas, and argued for their positions. During our interchanges, I decided that there was too much arguing, so I focused my attention and support on the one person who had managed to complete all of the tire rims. Since the two of us were the only team members in agreement, the others soon switched to our position. It was a forced choice in that there simply was not time to do otherwise. In this way, we came to a consensus.

The last task of the day was an individual problem-solving exercise. Applicants were given the following scenario: An assembly plant was having difficulties with product quality and employee morale. The applicant played the role of an outside consultant brought in as a problem solver to discover the source of the trouble and come up with a recommendation for action. We were each given a series of three-minute interviews with a plant representative. Between interviews there were five-minute periods to evaluate our information and come up with more questions. In the end, each applicant was to write up his or her recommendation for action. This exercise tested an individual's ability to focus on a problem and come up with some sort of solution, while under pressure of time and space constraints.

At the end of the day, we filled out new application forms and the coordinator fielded questions. In response to our questions we were told that SIA had already hired about three hundred associates. If we were offered jobs, we could start immediately. If we heard anything right away, it would be bad news. Good news would take ten days to two weeks. Imagine my surprise when, four days later, I received an evening phone call scheduling me for a physical at a local health clinic and an interview at the plant.

The physical began at 8:30 A.M. and continued for more than three hours. The first step was a drug and alcohol test. In order to protect the "chain of custody," a nurse observed while I urinated into a cup and we both witnessed the sealing of the vial by initialing it. When I asked her if she also observed male applicants, she said, "No, the doctor does them." In addition to being tested for drugs and alcohol, I was tested for hearing, lung capacity, vision, and color blindness, and given a brief physical examination. I thought that was the end of it but there were still more lab tests. Blood was drawn and another urine sample collected. As I left the lab, I scrutinized my billing sheet—$118. It was my understanding that this was paid for by the state of Indiana as part of the financial incentive package offered to SIA for locating in Indiana. When I questioned other SIA workers, I found that they were generally unaware of this arrangement. They believed that SIA was footing the bill.

My interview was scheduled for four o'clock the same day. I drove through the main plant gate and a guard called the security office for clearance. He gave me a pass for my car and a visitor's badge. When I entered the plant, I was given another security check and was then escorted to a small room where I waited to be interviewed.

There were two separate interviews, the first with a woman team leader from Body Assembly. When she left, two male team leaders, one from Body Assembly and the other from the Trim and Final department, came into the room and asked many of the same questions. Questions were prewritten so that all applicants were asked the same ones and the team leaders wrote down all responses.

Sometimes I responded in terms of my experiences with factory jobs from previous years. If the question concerned a specific time period, I answered in terms of the job I was doing at that time. The following is a sampling of what I was asked during the interviews:

1. Describe two decisions that you are glad you made in the last six months.
2. Describe the last meeting you attended with fellow employees.
3. Name the things you hate and like the most about your current job.
4. Explain your career goals.
5. What is the last thing you repaired?
6. What qualities do you have which you feel prepare you to be an Associate?

7. Name two things you've done which benefited fellow employees.
8. Have you ever felt you had to change something that management ordered, or have you ever disagreed with management? Describe what it was.
9. Name two things that you have done on the job to improve it.
10. What safety equipment have you had to wear on the job?
11. Have you ever stopped a fellow employee from violating safety rules?
12. Have you ever had to violate a safety rule?
13. Why do you want to be an Associate?
14. What is the most difficult group of people you have ever had to work with?
15. What do your parents think about you working in a factory?

Since the team leaders used the same set of questions and wrote down our responses, one might wonder why they bothered with an interview format. They could as easily have given each applicant the list and had us write answers. Most likely, SIA wanted to see what we looked like and whether or not an applicant appeared to fit in. There was some evidence to support this contention. The following example shows a clear gender subtext to fitting in at SIA. When I was working in the plant, I asked one team leader if anyone had actually been turned down (by this team leader) at the interview stage. The reply was: "Only one. I turned down a woman who was just too attractive. I was afraid that the men wouldn't be able to keep their minds on their work." In this case, it was obviously nothing that the applicant said or did in the interview; she simply did not fit that team leader's image of an Associate.

Worker Reaction to Selection

When I discussed the employment selection process with other SIA workers in the weeks after I was hired, I found many were amazed that they had actually been hired after their interviews. They expressed a feeling that the interviews seemed antithetical to the rest of the process. Workers complained that even after they had successfully completed all the objective hurdles found in the GAT and Phase I and Phase II, the ultimate test rested on a subjective interview. One worker expressed frustration that, since each stage evaluated workers on the basis of new criteria, "a person might be the most outstanding candidate to ever come out of Phase I and Phase II, slip up at the interview, and they are out the door." Others said they had expected something different, that their success in the testing process might have carried more weight. Instead, each step was simply part of a long, drawn-out process of elimination.

Workers generally recognized that the hiring process functioned as a gatekeeper. There was widespread sentiment that SIA used it to weed out undesirables. People were not, however, in total agreement as to what constituted an undesirable. One worker thought the process was an effort to screen out anyone not willing to be cooperative. She said that you could not pass the team exercises in Phase I unless you were willing to cooperate with others. Another said that the GAT cut out anyone who was not intelligent. A third worker said that SIA was trying to get rid of "freeloaders." He thought that the timed assembly tasks in Phase II and the film showing what it was like to work in a Japanese assembly plant (I was not shown this film) were both aimed at "scaring away anyone who wasn't willing to work." One thing that everyone agreed on was that SIA wanted people with good work habits. If anyone was late for one of the phases of the selection process, the employment coordinator informed us, that person's "chance at a job was gone."

One worker was pretty certain the whole selection process was aimed at exposing union supporters. Particularly, he felt the content of the questionnaire in Phase I "would single out union sympathizers, or at least people who did not believe that what was good for the company was necessarily good for them." It was considered common knowledge that SIA was antiunion. One of the women in my orientation class asked another member during a break what he felt about the union. He said that according to the workers he had talked with, SIA did not want a union. (During this period there was a well-publicized organizing campaign at Nissan, another Japanese transplant. The union lost the vote by a two to one margin. The fact that the campaign was current stimulated union discussions during breaks.)

Only two workers out of the more than forty I questioned appeared not to be cynical about the hiring process. One believed it was "fantastic," describing how he felt that for once, it had given him the opportunity to be fairly evaluated. Since the process involved much more than simply filling out an application and hoping for an interview, he said, "it gave guys like me, who didn't know the right people, a chance." He said that SIA had actually "tapped into his potential" and that the observers "had really gotten to know him through the tests."

The reactions of training class members to the selection process ran from "grueling" and "demanding" to "fun" and "ridiculous." Everyone agreed, however, that they had never worked so hard to land a job. The general sentiment was that we had really accomplished something and were among a select few. In training and during screening we were constantly made aware of our unique status. Subaru-Isuzu Automotive had chosen us out of thirty thousand applicants.

In addition to feeling special because of being among a select few, applicants had their hopes and expectations steadily raised by the long and drawn-out nature of the process. After every step applicants were instructed to wait for a letter to be notified of their chances. As one described it, "It was like riding an emotional roller coaster." Not everyone was able to see the process through to the end. It took me more than six months to get hired. I filled out an application on February 3 and started work July 10, and this after a diligent effort at keeping my application up to date with weekly calls to the DET office just to make certain I was still in the computer. Not everyone took six months but many waited even longer. The quickest hire that I was aware of took nine weeks.

Not only were applicants eliminated by low scores at each phase of the screening, but the fact that hiring was broken down into several separate phases encouraged a process of self-elimination. For example, four of the twelve scheduled applicants failed to show up for the GAT and only sixteen of twenty attended Phase I. Completing the process demanded perseverance. This structure enabled SIA to select from the large pool of prospective workers those with the greatest desire and determination. Workers had to be highly motivated to submit to aptitude tests, to being observed and evaluated, and to undergoing physical examination and the personal intrusion of urinalysis.

In order to maintain their status in the selection process, most applicants were forced to make some degree of sacrifice. Since most were currently employed, they were forced to take several days off work, without pay, in order to participate. Many reported that their employers were not pleased with granting them time off to apply for another job. In addition, several applicants reported that they lived in another state or a long distance from the recruitment and training center. Participating in selection meant that they would have to spend a night away from home, or begin driving to the test site early in the morning, arrive back home late that night, and wake up exhausted for their regular jobs. However, all of these hardships only seemed to increase the desire to succeed and to heighten the sense of accomplishment when one did succeed. The result was a mix of positive feelings toward the company for being chosen. After all, the company was willing to go to great lengths to find the "very best" and applicants certainly felt they were the best, having outscored thirty thousand others and outsmarted the observers.

On the other hand, I found that many workers seemed to believe they had succeeded because they were smart, not because they were team players. During Orientation and Training, several workers acknowledged that they "really were not team players" and would "rather work alone if given the choice." Others commented that they knew they had to behave cooperatively with the other applicants in order to get the job—especially during the team scenarios—even though they felt like doing just the opposite. In various ways, workers expressed the fact that they had figured out how to beat the system. This is similar to Fucini and Fucini's (1990) findings concerning worker reaction to the selection process at Mazda.

At SIA, most successful applicants appeared to have engaged in a kind of charade in order to gain access to employment. In comments to me, many shared a sentiment expressed by one particular worker that "right from the start, I knew what the company was looking for." Workers admitted that they had not always been honest when filling out the questionnaire, especially in regard to their general feelings about supervisors. One person expressed it concisely: "I wanted the job and I was not going to blow my chances by really letting the company know how I felt."

There were several outside sources to alert an interested applicant as to what SIA expected of workers. The *Facts and Information* booklet at the DET special office explained the company's team philosophy. Before the plant opened, area newspapers ran feature articles focusing on the company's new style of management. Both sources stressed that SIA used a team concept relying on cooperation, safety, and quality. This information was reinforced by the employment coordinator when he informed us that less than half of participants passed Phase I, but almost all who went through Phase II were called for an interview. Therefore, Phase I was the critical gatekeeper. This was the phase that evaluated our behavior during team scenarios.

As one can see, workers' reactions to making it through the hiring process were complex. An obvious component in SIA's strategy was the duration and scheduling of the process. It provided the essential element for selecting the most motivated. A less obvious aspect was that even though the process was transparent to many workers, at the same time there was an underlying notion that it did have some integrity. Its quantitative nature (e.g., scoring applicants' statements) gave an impression of objectivity. In addition, the fact that so much money, time, and effort went into the selection of employees reinforced the belief that the company was willing to go to great lengths to select the best.

Ironically, the qualities that people designated necessary for successfully gaining employment were probably quite different from the qualities the company seemed to be seeking. Workers were intent on beating the system and many manipulated it through their charade. Successful applicants who followed the charade had to see past immediate and obvious demands in order to understand what it actually took to be noticed and "win" and were quite willing to manipulate the hiring process in order to succeed.

Theoretical Implications: Compliance or Resistance?

Management carefully structured every aspect of the process and in order to succeed, it was necessary for applicants to perform within a prescribed pattern of behaviors. However, it was within this prescribed pattern that applicants found a basis for resistance. Although workers were forced to comply with management's goals in order to get a job, their compliance was often only superficial, a kind of ruse. As noted, many applicants said they had tricked the company into hiring them. They seized the initiative and manipulated the process to their own end and, in doing so, were able to overcome the initial obstacle to employment.

The nature of the Japanese pre-employment screening process introduces a gatekeeping tactic to add to management's arsenal for increasing control on the shop floor. It potentially has both direct and indirect effects on shop floor behavior. The most obvious and direct effect is its gatekeeping function, predictably aimed at screening out potential union supporters—that is, those workers who view the employment relation as adversarial. Gatekeeping is achieved by selecting the applicants who appear to be most cooperative and motivated to work in a union-free SIA plant.

Indirectly, the screening can be seen as part of a longer term strategy aimed at establishing the parameters of behavior on the shop floor. This could arguably be accomplished through the socialization that occurs while the applicant is involved in screening. After successfully completing the hiring process, the applicant should have a clear understanding of the kind of behavior that will be expected on the shop floor. SIA is banking on the likelihood that if an applicant is willing to cooperate to get a job, he or she will continue to cooperate to keep it. Yet, worker response to the screening process may have a contradictory effect. As noted, worker resistance to screening procedures emerged in the form of a charade; however, if the charade continues on the shop floor, it may simply become a peculiar form of compliance, its potential for resistance never surfacing.

A key to untangling the complex nature of worker response and understanding the direction that it may take on the shop floor is to keep in mind that successful completion of the hiring process is not necessarily linked to team behavior being an essential part of one's personality. One merely has to have the savvy to understand what it takes to get through the selection and then be willing to play the game. As regards the effects of the selection process on the shop floor, participating in the charade potentially has both negative and positive effects for workers.

An unanticipated consequence of emerging successfully from screening is that the applicant may become an active participant in creating a "mobilization of bias" (Schattschneider 1960) on the shop floor, a bias that screens out behaviors not viewed as cooperative or supportive of the company's team. If management's intent is to establish team behavior as the norm, then each applicant who hires in as a team player assists in establishing that norm. One might argue that management has only to construct a process that gives applicants the opportunity to demonstrate their cooperative abilities and it is irrelevant whether or not a person actually possesses the qualities of a team player. Management can take comfort in the thought that whatever motivates workers to adjust their behavior to get jobs will continue to motivate them to keep these. Ultimately, without union representation, the nature of this mobilization of bias places the worker in a vulnerable position. If unconditional cooperation becomes the dominating form of shop floor culture, it can only serve to reinforce the company's ability to institute additional mechanisms to speed up and intensify work.

At the same time, however, the fact that the company's motives were transparent to many workers and that applicants were not totally taken in by the rhetoric of team participation suggests possibilities for future resistance. For example, many workers readily acknowledged their willingness to lie and trick the company through their charade. Furthermore, this form of resistance—manipulating the system to benefit one's own interest—may provide the basis for future resistance. The question is whether or not workers are able to attach terms and conditions to their willingness to cooperate. Whether or not the company is successful in structuring the behavior of its workers, as it is with the behavior of its applicants, remains to be seen. The ultimate test of the effectiveness of the screening process will be played out on the shop floor.

What has been the net impact of such a process? Based on a set of follow-up interviews that I conducted with workers during the spring of 1994, it is my assessment that the positive impact of pre-employment selection on workers' attitudes has decreased over time. Initially, the selection process was an important part of our psychological profile. Workers felt important for having been chosen and then making it through the hurdles of selection. Their feelings toward themselves and the company were reflected in their enthusiasm. I believe that the screening process was one of the variables leading to that initial enthusiasm.

Although workers continue to see themselves as important, it later seems to be related more closely to a status distinction within the workforce than simply to having achieved employment. The fact that Associates are permanent rather than temporary employees seems to be the salient factor, increasingly evident as the use of temporary workers has dramatically increased. The impact of using temporary workers has caused a dilemma for many Associates as they realize that their permanent status is due to the exploitation of temporaries working right next to them. There is an underlying feeling that the company is now "using" people, and a belief that Associates are no longer as important is beginning to surface.

In describing this shift in attitude, an Associate referred to the hiring process as a kind of measuring stick to convey a sensed change in how Associates were originally treated and how newly hired permanent employees are now being treated. Pre-employment screening has thus taken on a different meaning. It is now a hurdle for the temps who are already doing the work and have been exposed to the politics on the shop floor. A new workforce is emerging that seems to be operating under an atmosphere of intimidation instead of enthusiasm.

3

Orientation and Training

The type of orientation and training experienced by new workers entering a plant organized around the Japanese model is very different from what one would find in a traditional U.S. auto plant. In U.S. plants, training has traditionally been job specific, containing no behavioral or philosophical components. Typically, new workers are simply given a pamphlet outlining wages, benefits, and work rules. Then they are put on the shop floor to watch another worker perform the job that they will do (Fucini and Fucini 1990:66). In their research on Japanese-owned factories in the United States, Hodson, Hooks, and Rieble found training was largely restricted to communication skills, team orientations, and indoctrination in the company's philosophy (1992:288). In the Big Three, an average of 46.4 hours is spent in training new production workers compared to an average of 370 hours in the Japanese auto transplants (Womack, Jones, and Roos 1990:92).

At SIA the weeks in Orientation and Training created an ideological bridge between the pre-employment selection process and working as a team member in the plant. Orientation and Training provided us with a common base of knowledge about the company, introduced us to company philosophy, included segments directed at behavior, and equipped us with a minimum baseline of technical training. Our instruction contained both technical and attitudinal components. The technical component included the practical aspects of becoming an employee and comprised about fifty-six hours of our total instructional time of 127.5 contact hours. Ironically, I found these classes to be of little direct value in the plant. They tended to be overly general, mostly video presentations, and no attempt was made to link them to our immediate situation.

The attitudinal or values-oriented component was aimed at socializing us into becoming "good Associates." The relative importance of this dimension of our orientation and training is reflected by the fact that it occupied just over seventy-one hours of the total instructional time. Socialization also took place continuously as we formed friendships with classmates during our lunches, breaks, and each morning before class. We had classes explaining SIA history and philosophy, "kaizening," a program called Cross Cultural Training, and safety lectures. Further classes covered interaction, production organization, learning enhancement, and quality philosophy, and there were periodic tours of the plant. All of these classes were aimed at socializing the new worker into SIA's way of doing things. The most basic component shaping our attitudes involved the process of developing friendships with other classmates. As our orientation instructor told us: "Get to know each other well, because you'll be spending the next twenty years together."

The bonds formed with classmates created a connectedness that continued on the shop floor. After we entered the plant, these friendships were often sustained on a daily basis. Classmates met in the cafeteria for lunch and went out together on weekends. If the socializing that took place during breaks and informally was also included in the time devoted to the attitudinal component (e.g., we were given about fifteen minutes' break nearly every hour), it would be even greater than seventy-one hours. As Hodson et al. (1992) found, socialization was the most important factor in our Orientation and Training experience. The bonds we formed were very effective in providing for a smooth transition into the plant. The camaraderie also seemed to make the transition to identifying with one's team that much easier.

All new employees, whether clerical, management, or production workers attend one week of orientation followed by two weeks of classroom training. During this time we were paid our usual rate of pay at forty hours per week. A few of the job assignments required extra time in training. Workers assigned to the Paint department were given three additional weeks of training and welders attended a week of welding classes at the local technical school. During the three weeks of Orientation and Training, our days began at 8:30 A.M. and ended at 5:00 P.M. The following is an approximate schedule of the first three weeks:

Week One: Orientation

Monday	8:30	Socializing with class members
	9:00	Welcome to SIA
	9:30	Description of payroll and benefits

	12:00	Lunch
	12:30	Introduction to SIA (history of company)
	2:30	Description of security at SIA
	3:30	Safety and hazards communication
	4:30	Job Training Partnership Act screening (only for those few who qualified for Indiana job training funds)
Tuesday	8:30	Uniform fitting
	9:00	Cross-cultural training
	12:30	Lunch
	1:00	Spacetronics (group lesson in kaizening)
Wednesday	8:30	Socializing with class members
	9:00	Winning through interaction (behavior training)
	12:00	Lunch
	1:00	One-on-one interactions (behavior training)
Thursday	8:30	Socializing with class members
	9:00	Work rules and guidelines
	10:00	Sexual harassment prevention
	11:00	Kaizen
	12:00	Lunch
	1:00	Production organization and method
	2:00	Plant tour
Friday	8:30	Socializing with class members
	9:00	Handling conflict (behavior training)
	12:00	Lunch
	1:00	Group interactions (behavior training)

Week Two: First Week of Training

Monday	8:30	Socializing with class members
	9:00	Learning enhancement
	12:00	Lunch
	1:00	Learning enhancement
Tuesday	8:30	Socializing with class members
	9:00	Learning enhancement
	12:00	Lunch
	1:00	Learning enhancement

Wednesday	8:30	Socializing with class members
	9:00	Mainframe computer
	9:30	Fire and spills
	12:00	Lunch
	1:00	Introduction to Statistical Process Control
Thursday	8:30	Socializing with class members
	9:00	Blueprint reading
	12:00	Lunch
	1:00	Blueprint reading
Friday	8:30	Socializing with class members
	9:00	SIA quality philosophy
	10:00	Sketching
	12:00	Lunch
	1:00	Sketching

Week Three: Second Week of Training

Monday	8:30	Socializing with class members
	9:00	Hazardous wastes
	10:00	Basic lubrication
	11:00	Voluntary (preventive) maintenance
	12:00	Lunch
	1:00	Production safety
Tuesday	8:30	Socializing with class members
	9:00	Operation Instruction Sheet training
	12:00	Lunch
	1:00	Operation Instruction Sheet training
Wednesday	8:30	Socializing with class members
	9:00	Basic car engineering
	12:00	Lunch
	1:00	Basic car engineering
Thursday	8:30	Socializing with class members
	9:00	Basic car engineering
	12:00	Lunch
	1:00	Basic car engineering
Friday	8:30	Socializing with class members
	9:00	Basic hand tools
	12:00	Lunch
	1:00	Basic hand tools

Each morning, the first half-hour was spent socializing with class members while the training staff met. We had many breaks. There were fifteen-minute breaks between most classes and if a class lasted several hours, we often had a break every hour. During breaks, we usually gathered in groups outside the training center while some class members smoked or drank soft drinks and coffee.

Orientation

July 10 was my first day at SIA. I received a telephone call from the company the last week in June telling me to arrive at the plant before 8:30 A.M. and check in with the security guard at Gate Two. The guard directed me to the security office in the main building where I picked up a temporary identification badge. Three other new employees (one woman and two men) came into the office while I was waiting for my badge. After signing in and receiving our badges, we left the main plant and crossed a small parking lot to the training building.

The training building was of simple construction—a rectangular building with aluminum roof, doors, and siding. As we entered the building my eyes were drawn to several large photographs on the south wall, opposite the door. Groups of American team leaders were pictured during their several weeks of training in Japan; many of them were dressed in Japanese clothing and headbands. Nearly all of them were white men. The east wall of the entry way was covered with charts designating instructors and classes for each room for every day of the month. A doorway on the west wall led to the instructors' office.

I was immediately struck by the furniture arrangement in the office. All the desks were pushed together in the middle of the room and there was no indication as to which desk belonged to the head person. There was a small refrigerator in the office and a man offered to put my lunch there. He then directed me to the Trooper room where the orientation sessions were held.

From the southeast corner of the entry way, a hallway led to a break area with vending machines and several classrooms, each named for a Subaru or Isuzu vehicle. The four of us entered the Trooper room and, because the room was full, one of the instructors brought an additional table and chairs. There was a writing board at the front of the room and a map of Japan. Three people sat at each table, facing the front. Even though it was only 8:25, the four of us were the last to arrive. Several class members had been waiting for more than thirty minutes. People were nervous and excited. This was a very unusual way to begin a new factory job.

One of the several instructors opened the class with a few jokes and then grew serious as he told us how lucky we were to have been hired by SIA. He was adept at handling the class and the class appeared to like him. They laughed at his jokes and freely interacted with him. A few months later, a worker referred to him as a womanizer, telling me that he had flirted with her openly in class. She said she told him that she was married and even though he said he was also married, he continued to flirt with her. He finally stopped after she refused to respond, she said, and he proceeded to direct his attention to another young woman in her class. Ironically, he was one of the instructors who delivered the lecture on sexual harassment later that week. His actions communicated a mixed message about sexual harassment; his behavior indicated a tolerance for practices which belied the content of his future lecture.

Apparently, it was customary for the training instructors to go out drinking after work and they usually invited members of the classes. Each morning class members routinely listened to complaints of the instructors' hangovers. Their drinking habits became a topic of discussion during breaks. "It seems rather ironic that the instructors are so open about their drinking exploits when the company has such a strong antidrug stand—after all, we had to pass a drug test to work here," said one of my classmates. When class members began working in the plant, we learned that there was a double standard applied to drug use. Getting intoxicated at company parties was widely accepted and even encouraged. At the same time we were asked to wear buttons in support of a local antidrug campaign.

There were forty people in our orientation class. Usually orientation classes are half that size but this one was doubled up because the July 4 holidays fell in the previous week. Eight of us were women and everyone was white. The instructor had us introduce ourselves with a description of where we had worked or gone to school. As we talked, he would find something in what each person said and tease us, which made the class laugh and feel more comfortable.

Eight class members had degrees from the local university (three were new graduates), three worked as farmers, two were computer programmers, two recently retired from the army, another had just finished four years in the navy, and one had been a golf course attendant. There was a school teacher, day care worker, manager in a snack food plant, park caretaker, psychiatric ward orderly, grocery store manager, IRS investigator, bank clerk, an engineer (hired as such for SIA), and a supervisor at an automobile plant (hired as a group leader at SIA), and the remaining thirteen had previous factory experience. Only one person had actually worked in an auto factory, a stamping plant. Four were from out of state—New York, Illinois, Georgia, and Kentucky. During the second week, I suggested that we break into groups according to our age and discovered that, at thirty-nine, I was oldest person in the class.

My field notes indicate that most of my classmates either expressed antiunion sentiment or said nothing about the union. Excerpts from my field notes during orientation and training illustrate what appeared to be collective sentiments concerning the union; all names used are false. These expressions of union sentiment flowed out of informal conversations. The first two examples represent workers' fears of unions, expressing a standard reaction which associates unions with strikes and adversarial labor relations:

> At lunch . . . just about everyone at the table expressed
> antiunion sentiment. Teresa worked in management for 17
> years at a factory. She said: "If a union comes in, you have to
> fight for everything because management refuses to
> cooperate." One of the women had worked at the post office
> and she said she was forced to join the union. She said: "If a
> union strikes, you have to go out and then you are weeks
> without a pay check." (July 12, 1989)

> Terry said, "I hope that the organizers won't be at the gate
> bothering us," and Dave expressed the same concern. (July
> 28, 1989)

The general antiunion sentiment that was verbalized by many workers in the plant is reflected in the next excerpt. It seemed as though workers were eager to let others know of their stance against unions:

> At one of our afternoon breaks I talked again to Bob (the
> worker from Body) and also to Sandy, who worked at the
> UAW plant. Bob asked Sandy if he was able to vote on the
> UAW coming into the plant today, how would he vote? Sandy
> said he would vote no "because I was laid off because of the
> UAW and those with more seniority, but who weren't as good,
> stayed on." Bob said, "That's the way the whole plant is. No
> one wants a union." (July 14, 1989)

A further excerpt is representative of antiunion workers attempting to explain away why anyone might vote for union representation:

> There was talk about the Nissan defeat over the UAW. Teresa said: "The people who voted for the union probably just did it because their husbands belonged, or for reasons like that." Dick said: "If management treats its workers right, there is no reason for a union." (July 28, 1989)

General Areas of Learning

Activities during orientation, as the schedule for that week indicates, covered three general subject areas: Nuts and bolts—that is, information concerning benefits and pay schedules, work rules, uniform fittings, and plant tours; company history and philosophy; and behavior or attitude training.

Nuts and Bolts

This component, the shortest segment of training, began with a session on work rules, which I recorded thus:

> We are to call in when sick.
> Work begins at 6:30 A.M. and ends at 3:00 P.M.
> We will be given two ten-minute breaks per day.
> The assembly line is stopped during all breaks.
> At the start of each shift we will participate in a few minutes
> of exercises and then kaizening for ten minutes. During the
> kaizen sessions the team will discuss how to improve a
> specific job—changing it to be faster, safer, or result in
> better quality.

The rules were presented by one of the orientation instructors. Each rule was announced to us and a brief period was spent describing kaizen sessions.

A representative from the Human Relations department spoke to us concerning benefits and pay. She spent an hour detailing how to fill out our time cards (time clocks had not yet been installed) and describing the health and pension benefits. We were also fitted for uniforms and finally, the class was taken on plant tours to familiarize us with the operation. Our first tour lasted three hours and was right down on the shop floor; subsequent tours were conducted on the overhead walkway. We started in the stamping plant and covered each department with the exception of Paint. Everyone seemed excited during the tour. The plant was well lighted and quite clean with bright splashes of color from the yellow guard rails and orange robots.

SIA History and Philosophy

The session on SIA's history began with background on its parent companies. Class members learned that Subaru's parent, Fuji Heavy, was started in 1917. In 1919 it opened an aircraft company and from 1937 to 1945 it built military aircraft. After World War II it was split into twelve small companies. From 1945 to 1953 it was forced to stop building aircraft and, according to the instructor, was "directed to make consumer goods such as buckets, shovels, and rakes—small items to protect the U.S." (While discussing the World War II period, the instructor seemed skittish. He did not tell us who had directed the Japanese to make consumer goods.) In 1955 it began building cars. The logo, five stars within an oval band, is found on Subaru vehicles, the stars representing the five companies now controlled by Fuji Heavy. They manufacture cars and trucks, aircraft, trains, buses, and industrial engines. The circle surrounding the five stars represents the parent company.

We were then introduced to Isuzu's history. Isuzu began in 1910 with ship building. In 1935 it built a prototype bus. The company underwent several name changes until 1949 (the reason was not explained). General Motors affiliated with it in 1982 and now owns over 40 percent. The Chevy spectrum was built in 1984 and by 1986 more than three million had been exported to the United States. The company now has seven manufacturing facilities producing trucks, buses, and automobiles. Its company symbol, two vertical columns, represents harmony and employees working together. Both the Subaru and Isuzu history narratives also emphasized the symbolic representation of the ethos of cooperation.

The instructor went on to say that when the parent companies decided to engage in a joint venture in the United States, seven states competed to win the site: Indiana, Ohio, Arkansas, Illinois, Kentucky, Missouri, and West Virginia. He said that in December 1986 the joint venture chose Indiana due to its overall superiority in technology, community, schools, labor, highways, education, and money. In March 1987 SIA incorporated and broke ground in April of 1988. The first pilot car was produced on June 20, 1989. Start-up was scheduled for September 1989. Initially, in phase one, SIA planned to produce 120,000 vehicles per year (60,000 trucks and 60,000 cars). In 1989 the company began the first phase of production and phase two was to begin in June 1990 with the addition of a complete second shift. Vehicle production then was to double to 240,000 per year. For phase one, a total of 1,700 employees were to be hired (at this point SIA had hired about 500 in production) and the second phase was to bring the workforce to over 3,000. (As of the fall of 1993, the local newspaper reported that SIA still employed only about 1,900 Associates).

All of the instructor's narratives emphasized U.S. activities. The U.S. focus, including Indiana's special qualities, was probably an effort to prevent any Japanese backlash among Associates. Highlighting Indiana fit with the company's overall attempt to instill in Associates a sense of being part of something special, although learning that Indiana won out because of its "overall superiority" jarred somewhat in that Indiana ranks forty-sixth in the nation for the percentage of high school students who pursue higher education.

SIA philosophy was presented both formally and informally. Formally, we had regular class periods dedicated to teaching the content of SIA's company philosophy. Informally, we were given further understanding of the subject through testimonials from American instructors, department heads, and a vice president. Informal testimonials praising SIA's style of operation occurred throughout our week in orientation and continued during our two weeks in technical training. A common theme was that SIA was a caring company. For example, a lecture was delivered by the manager in charge of safety, who assured us that safety was part of company philosophy and that the number one priority at SIA was for Associates always to behave in a safe manner. He said that as a company, "SIA was exceptional with its strong emphasis on employee safety." On another occasion our orientation leader assured us that we had come to "a company which really cared about its employees." Other instructors claimed that this was the best place they had ever worked. The vice president of manufacturing told us how important we were to the organization and that through kaizen we "would always find a better way, as that was a Japanese management philosophy."

Formal lectures were presented to explain the details of the company's philosophy. A lecture on kaizening, for example, included a handout explaining the Kaizen Wheel: "It begins with an idea, then action, results, evaluation/standardization, and a return to another idea. A system of continuous improvement." Another training handout titled "Nanatsu-no Muda: 7 Wastes" listed matters to avoid:

1. Tsukurisugi—overproduction
2. Zaiko—inventory
3. Temachi—waiting
4. Unpan—conveyance (movement of parts)
5. Furyouhin-o tsukuru—making defective products
6. Dousa—motions (personal motion)
7. Koutei-sonomono—processing in itself
   Korera-no-muda-o-torinozoku-katsudou-ga-kaizen =
   Activities to eliminate these wastes called KAIZEN.

We were also given an untitled handout listing the seven principles of work:

1. Seiri—arrange, put in order
2. Seiton—tidy up, orderly, everything in its place, and everything goes in its place
3. Seisou—clean, to clean the plant site
4. Seiketsu—keep clean, keeping things where they belong and clean
5. Shitsuke—train, team discipline
6. Shitukari—intense training, priority
7. Situkoku—repeating the process

These principles fostered a work culture that differed from typical factory work in that they stressed orderliness, cleanliness, discipline, and training—a significant departure from a typical blue-collar factory culture where men assume a "manly" posture in relation to dirty, heavy tasks.

These handouts were read aloud to the class by the instructors, who seldom elaborated or explained, and there was no discussion or comment from class members. Trainees sat quietly as the information was read to them.

Behavior Training

In addition to the administrative aspects of working at SIA and company history and philosophy, the class was instructed on interaction through several three- and four-hour sessions of a video-driven program ("Interaction" by Development Dimensions International) based on the three KPs (key principles):

1. Maintain or enhance the other person's self-esteem.
2. Listen and respond with empathy.
3. Ask for help in solving the problem.

The program also included a list of interaction guidelines and a structure for group interaction which was described as especially useful when kaizening:

1. Describe what you want to talk about.
2. Gather and review the details.
3. Explore alternatives.
4. Agree on actions to be taken.
5. Agree to a follow-up time.

As a class member, I found both the presentation methods and the "Interaction" program itself condescending. The KPs and guidelines were repeated over and over again. Two class members even mentioned during a session that the techniques "should come in handy when trying to get our children to do things they don't want to." The program's underlying message was that, as Associates, we must be willing to conform when confronted with the requirement for change—after all, change was a basic kaizen principle. The message was presented through videotaped vignettes of American workers in factory settings. My impression was that the vignettes stereotyped older workers, presenting them as rigid and negative toward change. In a typical scene, a young worker would come up with an idea and then use the KPs and guidelines on an older, disgruntled worker. In the end, the savvy young worker would manage to convince the older worker to try the new approach. The older worker would begrudgingly consent after much convincing and would eventually be won over to the new way of doing things.

There was also a short presentation on SIA's organizational structure. The instructor told us that everyone, including managers, went through the same orientation classes. He described SIA as a very "flat" organization, meaning that there were few levels within management. The Operating Committee, the highest level of management within the plant, consisted of six people: the president, executive vice president of finance, senior vice president and controller, executive vice president of manufacturing and engineering, vice president of general affairs, and vice president of manufacturing. The last two were Americans; the president and the senior and two executive vice presidents were all Japanese. The instructor went on to say that below the Operating Committee were the manufacturing department managers for Stamping, Body, Paint, Trim and Final, Maintenance, Materials, and In Process Control (IPC). Below managers came the group leaders, then team leaders, and last, production Associates. Anyone who was not in production was referred to as a Staff Associate. Although the structure was presented as "flat," it was clearly hierarchical—consistent with traditional bureaucratic form; a shorter chain of command but a chain nonetheless.

Class members attended a two-and-a-half-hour class entitled "Cross-Cultural Training." The two instructors, a Japanese-American man and a young white woman, had both lived or spent time in Japan. They introduced class members to cultural diversity. We were shown a videotape with the message that American women and minorities would soon be a majority of the workforce. Therefore, it was necessary for industry to adjust to the differences and take advantage of "new ideas from new people."

Although the instructors were clearly enthusiastic about Japanese culture, they were not particularly successful in dispelling myths or stereotypes. Either they did not fully understand their subject or they themselves held stereotypes about us as workers. As a class member, I felt that the instructors believed we were incapable of understanding the concept of stereotyping or would be unwilling to change our views. Whatever the reason, the concept was not adequately explored and was at times presented in a glib manner.

The instructors showed the class a map of Japan and pointed out how because it was made up of islands, the country was very conservation minded. They listed some common stereotypes that Americans often held about the Japanese and then stereotypes that the Japanese often had concerning Americans. There was no discussion of any of these perspectives. Discussion was neither encouraged nor discouraged. We were told not to talk pidgin or broken English to the Japanese trainers because it would not help them learn to speak the language.

At the end of that day, as we were walking to our cars, two class members said they had found one of the cross-cultural training handouts offensive as it seemed to stereotype the Japanese. The handout, called "Salayman" (salary-man), comically illustrated some of the customs of

Japanese business executives. It might have been considered humorous to the Japanese; however, to those of us unfamiliar with their customs, its exaggerated form served to reinforce stereotypes.

To demonstrate Japanese business practices further and, more important, to drive home the egalitarian nature of the Japanese model, we were shown a videotape of the main office at SIA. The office seemed about the size of a football field and it contained row after row of desks. The cross-cultural instructors told us the video had been shot after hours, so the room was empty of people. All of the desks were empty of any papers or personal items. They said that the Japanese have a clean desk policy (nothing is to be left on one's desk at the end of the day) and that this is in keeping with their philosophy of orderliness. They went on to say that, in order to comply with the policy, many of the Americans put their things on their chairs and shoved them under their desks as they left at the end of the day. Unlike typical U.S. clerical workers, the Japanese kept their desks cleared of personal items.

The instructors called our attention to the arrangement of the office furniture as proof of the company's egalitarian philosophy. We were informed that the president and vice presidents of the company as well as all clerical workers and middle management had their desks in the same room. The desks of the American managers and their coordinators from Japan were pushed together so as to be touching.

After I began working in the plant, I was in the office on several occasions and found a definite order in where people were placed. The president and vice presidents were not simply scattered throughout the room. The president, Operating Committee members, and many of the department heads, such as the public spokesperson for SIA, were in the same row with their backs to the wall at the west end of the room—far from the noise and lineup at the copy machines. Engineers tended to be at the far north end, also away from the machines. Safety and benefits personnel were close to one of the main entry doors and clerical workers were scattered throughout the middle and east side, where the machines were located.

The cross-cultural training instructors informed the class that Japanese workers made very low monthly salaries, "hardly enough to live on." However, at the end of each year, they received an average of 5.3 months' wages as bonus pay. The class concluded with our learning some Japanese vowel and consonant sounds and then we wrote our names using the characters representing those sounds. The purpose of this exercise was not clear. The instructors did not cover words that we might use like *kaizen* or *muda* and there was no attempt to teach us frequently used words for communicating with our Japanese trainers. Instead, class members found that when working in the plant, we often communicated with our trainers by drawing pictures, using impromptu sign language, or speaking English. Possibly the instructors simply wanted to give us some idea of how difficult it was to learn another language so that we would respect the efforts made by our trainers.

On our final day of orientation, each class member received a pin and our class picture was taken (but we were not given a copy of the picture). Then came the moment we had all anxiously anticipated: we were given our job assignments. Four class members were assigned to the Materials department and because that department needed immediate help, they were to start work the following Monday. Seven were assigned to the Paint department and would receive additional special training. The four welders assigned to the Body Shop would also receive additional training in welding at the local technical school. The rest of us would work in Trim and Final. These assignments cut the number of class members by half to twenty for the next two weeks of training in technical fundamentals.

Training

The first two days of technical training consisted of a short course called "Learning Enhancement," specially designed for the automobile industry by our instructor, a professional educator from Dayton, Ohio. He told the class that his program had come about when General Motors began retraining some employees and found that workers hated the classes. According to the instructor, GM decided the problem was that workers had forgotten how to learn, which made the classes overly difficult. He was hired to teach workers learning techniques. His job at SIA, he told us, was to teach us to learn efficiently so that we would get the most out of our training. He taught us memorization techniques such as word association for recalling lists of items and for matching words to definitions. SIA planned to spend five percent of workers' time in ongoing training, he said.

The remainder of the two weeks was spent in basic classroom instruction. On day three we were given a brief overview of the mainframe computer controlling the assembly lines in the plant. Next, class members watched a videotape on what to do in case of fire or spills. (Interestingly enough, months later when I was working in the plant, there was a serious gasoline spill on the final line. We found the instruction to be of little use when confronted with an actual spill of any magnitude. When the spill occurred, no one knew what to do. It took several minutes before management made the decision to evacuate the building. In the meantime, gasoline was spraying out of one of the hoses on the final line directly across from my area.)

Later that day we received an introduction to Statistical Process Control (SPC), which is used for measuring consistency in product quality. We were also introduced to the Deming management method, which we were told was SIA's philosophy of management. The instructor told us Dr. W. Edward Deming was an American statistician who had revitalized Japanese industry after World War II and had been responsible for the kaizen philosophy. (Deming died in December 1993). We were given a handout listing the fourteen points that Deming claimed were necessary for a business to remain competitive:

1. Create consistency of purpose for improvement of product and service.
2. Adopt a new philosophy.
3. Cease dependence on inspections to achieve quality.
4. End the practice of awarding business on the basis of price.
5. Improve constantly and forever every process for planning, production, and service.
6. Institute training on the job.
7. Adopt and institute leadership.
8. Drive out fear.
9. Break down barriers between staff areas.
10. Eliminate slogans, exhortations, and targets for the work force.
11. Eliminate numerical quotas for the work force and numerical goals for management.
12. Remove barriers that rob people of pride of workmanship.
13. Institute a vigorous program of education and self improvement.
14. Put everybody in the company to work to accomplish the transformation. The transformation is everybody's job.

Class members were not encouraged to discuss the Deming handout.

We were then given a lecture on "Deming's Seven Deadly Diseases." The instructor's explanation about each disease is included in parentheses, and we were told that the last two refer only to the United States:

1. Lack of constancy of purpose
   ("No long range plans")
2. Emphasis on short term profits
   ("Undermines quality")
3. Evaluate by performance or merit, or an annual review of performance or merit
   ("Deadly effect on teamwork, breeds resentment")
4. Mobility of management
   ("Need to be able to make long range plans")
5. Running the company on visible figures alone
   ("Look at satisfied customers and attitude of workers")
6. Excessive medical costs
7. Excessive cost of warranties fueled by lawyers' contingency fees

There was no discussion other than the instructor's brief comments. Deming's model constituted a kind of official dogma.

The fourth day was spent learning to read a variety of blueprints at a superficial level. Part of the fifth morning was spent reviewing SIA's quality philosophy: "SIA's mission is to manufacture and sell quality vehicles, and thus to contribute to society through the growth of our company. . . . Quality is the top priority at SIA. . . . anything concerning quality must come first. Quality comes before production. If there is a quality problem, our manufacturing line must stop immediately. Only after solving and correcting the problem will we allow the line to be re-started" (*SIA Associate Handbook* 1989:10–11). During the quality lecture, instructors explained that there were red and yellow cords all along the line that Associates could pull when they had a problem. When the cords were pulled, the line would stop.

The rest of the day we worked on sketching. The instructor took us into the plant to Body assembly where we sketched robots and machinery. He said that the reason so much time is spent on sketching is because it is used in the plant to communicate with the trainers.

After sketching, class members were given another handout which, we were told, covered SIA's philosophy of management. It was presented to us very briefly and once again with little explanation. It seemed as though the instructor himself did not clearly understand the intent behind each principle. The company generated many documents describing its philosophy toward its workers. However, even while in training, I questioned whether or not the thinking expressed there was put into practice because none of the instructors seemed certain as to the meaning of the documents. The ten principles of SIA management philosophy follow with the instructor's comments in parentheses.

1. SIA is made up of its people—*We* are the corporation.
   ("In Japan a company would not do anything to hurt their people, so there are no unions or OSHA.")
2. Together, we must beat the competition.
   ("We must bring the whole team up together.")
3. Job security is important to all of us.
   ("There will be no layoffs during model changes.")
4. Quality is the top priority.
   ("Japanese trainers will only put out quality. One bad car will ruin a new plant.")
5. We must eliminate *muda* throughout the company.
   ("Waste")
6. Kaizen means searching for a better way.
   ("This is done through gradual small improvements.")
7. Each of us should strive to be a multitalented person.
   ("Versatility is the key to success.")
8. The spirit of SIA is enthusiastic involvement.
   ("Team work!")
9. Open communications build mutual trust.
   ("Driving out fear so you can talk to the person above you.")
10. We build Hoosier pride into every vehicle.
    ("These cars will go all over the world; we must show them that this state is a good place to work and live.")

The first three principles blur class distinctions through the use of the team metaphor. Use of the phrase "all of us" depicts the workforce as undifferentiated and with similar interests. Principles four through seven join the company and worker in a common goal, calling upon pride in one's work, pride in what is produced and in the process of production. Principles eight and nine and also seven build on the idea of team. SIA provides a nurturing environment, like a family, encouraging everyone to strive or stretch to be the best. This includes encouraging each Associate to nurture other team members to enter the fold through involvement in activities and by learning to trust group leaders. The last principle emphasizes SIA as American by highlighting Indiana and Hoosier pride. Again there was no discussion by class members.

My second and last week of training began with a videotape on hazardous wastes and their disposal. The video emphasized that SIA cared about the environment, its basic message being not to throw anything down the drain. (Ironically, once we were working in the plant, it became almost impossible for team members to dispose of hazardous waste. The team leader once put one of our teammates in charge of trying to get rid of a small can of turpentine left over from painting a ramp. The team member spent weeks searching for someone both authorized and willing to take the waste. Each person or department he consulted sent him on to another. He could find no one willing to handle a few cups of turpentine.)

Next we watched video about basic lubrication and voluntary maintenance, and then a third concerning production safety. All of these videos were general and classmates found that they had little application to our actual situation when we entered the plant.

We were told by many of the instructors that they were working on contract for SIA; therefore, they were temporary employees, not Associates. The temporary instructors included management students from the local university, instructors from the local technical school, and the education specialist for learning enhancement. The rest, including the orientation leader, were regular SIA employees—Staff Associates.

One particular instructor, a Staff Associate, gave us his testimonial on why he favored SIA as an employer. He said he had begun working for the company in February 1988 as one of the first thirty hired. Originally, he was not hired as an instructor but as a skilled die-maintenance Associate. He was sent to Japan for eighteen months of training. After three months, however, he injured his knee in a fall while trying to jump across a pit at the Japanese factory. "SIA believes that everyone has a place, so they found something else for me to do and put me in the training department," he said. He went on to say that "SIA is the best place I have ever worked and after twelve years in tool and die I have decided to stay with training."

As I gained more experience in working at the plant, I think I understood the basis for this trainer's sense of satisfaction with his job. Compared to working in the plant, life in the training center was probably a lot less stressful, certainly less physically demanding and safer, and definitely an improvement in hours and working conditions. Here was a skilled die maker who was training workers, not in tool and die but in what a great place SIA was. In the long run, his enthusiastic testimonials to new workers were probably of much greater use to the company than were his skills in tool and die.

On Tuesday of that week, we were trained in the use of the Operation Instruction Sheets. Operation Instruction Sheets provide exact details of every station and of each process within a station, including the parts, tools, safety precautions, and the exact amount of time it should take to implement each fragmented task. Whenever a job is changed, the operation sheets must be updated. We were told that they were the working source of knowledge about every job within the plant—a standardized description replicating what the worker does when performing each task. We also performed time and motion studies on each other. No one appeared to react negatively to timing others (even though this is a traditional method of speedup). That afternoon we had a kaizen exercise using the operation sheets. We were told to "brainstorm for process improvement."

Wednesday and Thursday were spent on classes in basic car engineering, including a description of a combustion engine. We also memorized the names of some parts of the car body. On Friday we examined basic hand tools, measuring devices, and impact wrenches, and performed an exercise in metricating standard U.S. measurements.

A recurring theme throughout Orientation and Training was the efficiency and dedication of Japanese workers as a model of what American workers should strive toward. For example, the orientation leader said: "The Japanese are very big on education and will be sending their children to the state capital for their sixth day of school each week." The head of the safety department said: "The Japanese are more safety conscious than Americans" and "The Japanese are more industrious and harder workers." Similarly, we were told that the Japanese method of doing many things was superior. There were probably several reasons for these messages and themes. They may have represented an attempt to instill in us a high level of respect for the Japanese trainers and the company philosophy. They also may have been intended as a motivational technique; creating competition with the Japanese was used as a motivating device in the plant. More than once our team leader, group leader, and even the car manager challenged us to "beat" the Japanese. Once our group leader told us that the company wanted us to produce a certain number of cars that day and that the "Japanese trainers didn't believe we could do it."

During one of the plant tours with our training class, the instructor called our attention to the fact that the Japanese trainers always stayed late and continued to work long after the American workers left for home. (The tour took place after the end of the regular shift.) On three different occasions, instructors emphasized that there was no occupational safety and health law in Japan. One instructor's explanation: "It is not necessary as the Japanese treat workers fairly." Another instructor said that Japan had no consumer protection or pollution laws to put a stranglehold on business, therefore they could be more competitive.

Finally, after several instructors had referred to how things were done in Japan, a class member spoke up with: "Just because they do it that way in Japan doesn't make it right." At that point the instructor backed off and agreed that this was true, saying, "I did not mean to make it sound that way."

This classmate's outburst was exceptional. During the course of Orientation and Training, there were only two other instances in which class members questioned or challenged instructors' statements. As new employees, we were in a vulnerable position. Until we were in the plant, we simply had to play along, as an excerpt from my notes illustrates. The second outburst during training came from me:

> During the Interaction segment we were asked for some feedback. I said that the program seemed kind of condescending as the leading characters in the videotaped vignettes tended to approach the other workers like children. The instructor had no idea how to respond to me. At the next break a class member took me aside to tell me that he "didn't agree with everything that was said either." One of the experienced workers in our class (if a department is in need of workers, some people go into the plant right after orientation and then come back later to finish their training with new hires) told me to "just go along with them, pretty soon you'll be in the plant." (July 12, 1989)

The advice to play along is similar to the charade that workers participated in during the hiring process. Once again, workers complied with company demands only on the surface. They relied on their wits to portray the necessary qualities that the company was expecting, all the while reassuring other workers that they were not the real "team players" that they appeared to be.

The third outburst was from a classmate worried about speedup. His challenge was in response to an in-class discussion about Nissan workers in Tennessee having voted two to one against union representation only a few days earlier. The discussion focused on the lack of necessity of unionizing at SIA. The instructor said, "Nissan had expanded from 200,000 to 400,000 vehicles per year and the employees were not properly trained to understand that sacrifices had to be made, but that the company would make up for it once the expansion was complete." He went on to say that "another example is GM's NUMMI plant. Their philosophy is to push the machines and people to the absolute maximum and then to pull back. This is the opposite of us (SIA)." It was then that our classmate responded with his concern over speedup and blurted out, "But where does it stop? They say we will build a car every fifty-seven seconds, but then it will be fifty." The instructor responded, "It never stops, but it will be because we open up more lines, not because you work that much faster."

Besides the instructors' remarks, some of the production workers expressed sentiments that the Japanese were special. The experienced worker in our class had worked at SIA for about three months. He said, "It takes the trainers a while before they trust you and see that you aren't stupid, but then you've got a friend for life." He also spoke highly of SIA's president and pointed him out to us in the cafeteria. Months later, however, I learned that the man he had pointed out was not the president but a member of the Operating Committee.

Anti-Japanese sentiment also surfaced during training. One instructor told us, "The Japanese are not creative in their thinking; they simply copy everyone else." He said he had observed this during his weeks in Japan. Clearly it was not a smart thing to say about one's employer, but I think he felt safe saying it to a room full of non-Japanese people, taking for granted that all of us would feel as he did.

Tensions regarding the Japanese model even surfaced among some of the instructors. There was a standing joke among the instructors about the inefficiency of Japanese team decision making. Referring to the posts in the plant that were to be painted a special color to indicate where fire equipment was located, an instructor would note: "It's been months and they still can't decide on the color or style." A comment often made was: "One thing you can depend on here is everything changes." The constant change in uniform styles was another topic of jokes as SIA had been through at least three styles by this time. Once an instructor jokingly told us: "If any of you guys get into trouble in there don't come crying to old 'Jerry-san' to come bail you out." Finally, one of the group leaders from the plant spoke to our class and, when describing the in-plant competition between the Japanese trainers on the Isuzu truck side and the trainers on the Subaru car side, said: "They fight like children and we have to serve as referees."

Training Ideals vs. Work Realities

The purpose of Orientation and Training was expressed by the instructors in different ways but all had a common theme—to create a cooperative workforce willing to conform to company demands. One instructor said that "training at the same level and background gives us all a common starting point." Referring to the training that team and group leaders received in Japan, one instructor said, "They sent people to Japan not to learn the job, but to educate them in a mental attitude of team work. . . . The main objective is to absorb the culture." Another instructor said he had been "told by three sources that the training department at SIA is on the leading edge of industrial education." He went on to say, "SIA wants us to understand the entire process so that we don't become adversarial employees." He then referred to the Nissan union vote and added, "There is a small number of disgruntled employees there who were not properly trained like us."

A clear message class members received during Orientation and Training was that at SIA everyone was equal and the company was concerned about its Associates—we would be just like one big family. We were told that as workers, we were more important to SIA than workers were to their American companies and Associates would always have input in decisions.

Class members found that the messages presented to us during Orientation and Training often were quite different from the reality of working in the plant. In fact, we were warned of this by two Associates from the plant who had joined our training class. "There is a big difference between what the instructors say the plant will be like and how it actually is," they told us. They said the plant was not very team spirited. "There is a power struggle between the car and truck trainers and it ends up screwing up our schedules and we have to put in overtime to make up for it."

Another contradictory message came from safety representatives. Class members were told that there would be "two or three safety reps out in every department with the authority to correct unsafe situations." After having heard so many statements about how egalitarian the company was, we naively thought that the safety representatives would be workers like us, but that was not the case. The reps were group leaders and a few team leaders, all appointed by management.

Class members' biggest surprise upon entering the plant concerned kaizening. During training, we had been led to believe that worker input would be constant and valued. This simply was not the case. Instead, it was as the three-month veteran worker had told us during a break: "I never kaizened yet!" Instructors had claimed that there would be a ten-minute kaizen meeting every morning. In reality (particularly after official production began), the meeting consisted of a five-minute quality report on the previous day's production. The team leader would pass around the report and sometimes a graph reflecting quality errors over a longer period of time.

In the plant a worker from another team responded to my question as to what he thought of the three weeks of Orientation and Training with the remark that his team was nothing like training instructors had said it would be. In reference to his team leader, he said, "It's Dick's way, or the highway."

A further contradiction involved the idea that there was truly two-way communication within the plant. The instructors stressed that management "really listens to everyone at SIA. . . . Communication is not only from the top down; it turns around and goes from the bottom up." Ironically, an area of contention concerning shift rotation surfaced in the plant while we were still in training. It aptly illustrates the top-down direction that at least some of the workers believed to be the case at SIA.

> At lunch I talked with Lori and Meg. They are two women in Materials. . . . They have been working in the plant for 6 weeks. They said that there is a big difference between what they teach us that the plant will be like in training and what it actually is. . . . Concerning swing shift: Lori and Meg said that when they were hired, they were told: "The shift we hired on would be the shift that we work." They talked to their group leader about having to swing when second shift starts,

but he said: "It is not open for discussion." They told me,
"The company only takes input from Associates on subjects
the company chooses." (July 17 and 18, 1989)

One of the experienced workers considered one aspect of the team
concept was very positive: "No one yells at anyone, they talk it out."
However, when this same worker discussed the American managers, he
expressed a definite them vs. us attitude. At lunch, a classmate said to
him that the vice president of manufacturing (an American) seemed like
a "nice enough guy." He replied, "You heard where he was from, right?
You don't spend twenty-three years at GM and then change your spots."
He went on to say, "All the front line is like him. A lot of them are old
GM management and there is no equality there." He smiled. "It must
have knocked the managers down a few pegs when they saw their offices." He clearly had no respect for the Americans who were in management positions, but the Japanese were a different story. When he had
pointed out to us the Japanese person he thought was the company president, he said, "He's not in the shop much, but seems OK." I do not
know how many former GM management employees were at the plant.
It seemed that many of the group leaders and nearly all department managers were from the auto industry. I knew several had worked at Volks-
wagen and also at GM. Despite SIA training and philosophy, it was
difficult to conclude that the corporate culture from those plants was not
impinging—in some ways—on the cooperative atmosphere at SIA.

The experienced workers in our class countered much of what the
instructors were telling us. Notably, this nearly always happened during
breaks—workers kept their mouths shut during class. When they told us
about what was happening in the plant, most of the time, it was to let us
know that they knew the score. However, the issue of shift rotation was
different. In that case they were trying to win us over to their side and
get us to agitate as soon as we entered the plant. People talked about
"sticking together on this one."

The company's decision to mix experienced with the inexperienced
workers thus had contradictory effects. At times, intermixing effectively
"debriefed" many of the new Associates. The experienced workers' interpretation of company behavior was often nearly opposite of what the
instructors led us to believe. It clearly worked against our socialization
to the company's philosophical position.

In summary, the success of the formal classroom training in shaping
our attitudes was mixed at best and was partially a reflection of the low

level of understanding that was demonstrated by most of the training instructors. Ironically, the company's ability to socialize its own instructors was, apparently, less than successful. Their limited understanding of the company's philosophical position—or possibly they did understand it but saw it as false—and the lack of sensitivity reflected in instructors' jokes concerning the Japanese way of doing things seem to indicate that many of the instructors were not committed to the Japanese approach. Perhaps it is impossible to rationalize a system thoroughly enough to get everyone on board.

As a component in SIA's overall scheme for gaining control on the shop floor, Orientation and Training was most effective for easing transition into the plant and for aiding workers in the process of identifying with teammates and for identifying themselves as members of the team. The bonds that we formed with Orientation and Training classmates were our first identifiable, human connection with the company. In previous factory jobs, fear and alienation had been my emotions on my first day on the shop floor. At SIA this simply was not the case. The atmosphere was friendly. I believe that there were three obvious reasons for that friendliness: everyone had gone through the same process to get there, providing us with a common experience; we already felt connected through the friends we had made; and the company would be choosing second shift team leaders from the existing workforce, so all workers were on their best behavior.

4

The Work Setting

Life on the assembly line, whether operated under the Japanese model or under traditional U.S. methods, continues to be a monotonous grind. However, there is one critical difference between the two systems: a key feature of the Japanese model is speedup and work intensification (Berggren 1992; Kamata 1982; Parker and Slaughter 1988). This chapter describes SIA's process of vehicle production with its flat management structure and rigid work process built on extensive Taylorist principles. An immediate and widespread effect of the Japanese model was physical injury, injuries which reached beyond the plant floor to touch the personal lives of the workers.

The Subaru–Isuzu plant spans more than fifty acres, and Trim and Final occupies about one-third of that area. Trim and Final has a "car side" where the Subaru Legacy is assembled and a "truck side" where Isuzu trucks are built. I worked in the Trim and Final department as a member of Team 1 in "trim one" on the car side. We were the first team to work on the bodies after they came out of Paint. About fourteen teams assembled the cars and a few more than fourteen worked on the truck side. The rest of the teams were in final inspection or in In Process Control (IPC), neither of which is directly connected to the main assembly lines.

The car side of Trim and Final consists of four areas: trim one, trim two, chassis, and final (see figure 1). Trim one and two runs the full length of the department, about the distance of a couple of city blocks. It takes several minutes to walk from one end to the other. There are four teams in trim one and two teams in trim two. Trim installs virtually everything inside the passenger compartment except for the seats, carpet-

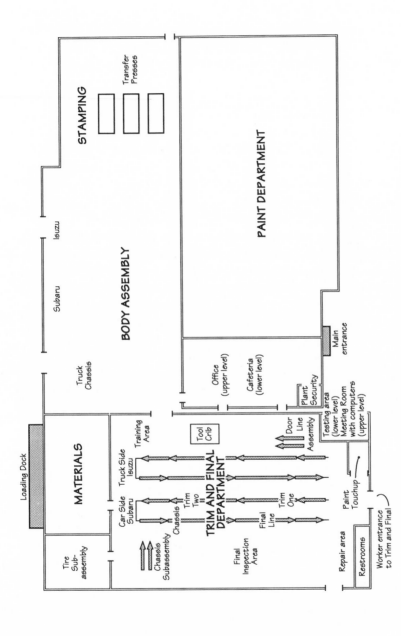

Figure 1. Layout of plant with detail of Trim and Final Department

ing, and steering wheel. It also assembles the doors and attaches a few items to the engine compartment.

Since both the truck and car lines run the length of Trim and Final and then back again, Team 1 is located between the final line on the truck side and the final line on the car side. We were the first team to work on the cars and, at the same time, we watched as they were driven off the line, as finished products.

As noted earlier, a relatively flat management structure exists at SIA with only a few levels of authority between the worker and the Operating Committee—the highest level decision-making body in the plant. As indicated in chapter three, the Operating Committee consists of the president and five vice presidents. Below them are six department managers—one for Trim and Final—and below managers are group leaders, team leaders, and production Associates.

In Trim and Final, salaried workers consist of nine group leaders, one car line manager, a truck line manager, and a single department manager. The team leaders are hourly employees. There were twenty-nine teams in all of Trim and Final, each with one team leader, and the average team size was seven. In 1989, the first year of production, Associates' pay started at $11.60 per hour and team leaders received $12.15 per hour. The following year production Associates' wages were raised to $12.49 and those of team leaders to $13.14. (As of February 1994, Associates with seniority dates equal to mine were making about $16.35 per hour.)

The department manager was not usually present on the floor, so the car and truck managers acted as "foremen." Group leaders worked as the managers' assistants and as troubleshooters for their teams. Team 1's group leader had four teams under his control: Team 1 and Team 2 on the main assembly line and two teams which assembled the doors on a separate, smaller line. Most group leaders had three or four teams under them. However, two of the nine group leaders in Trim and Final were engineers who directed no teams. In addition to those nine, there was a group leader from Human Resources who worked as a liaison between that department and Trim and Final. Since the Human Resources group leader and the engineers directed no teams, their designation was misleading. For them, it was more an indication of wage and organizational rank than a description of their jobs.

On the car side, the fourteen teams were broken down into sixty-nine stations on both sides of the line. Team members referred to the stations and the people working them as though they were same. In other words, when team members referred to the work I performed, it was the work done by "one left"; however, team members did not refer to each other by station when away from the line. Team 1 was divided into twelve stations, six to a side. Eventually, one person would be responsible for each station. When I left, we were still short one person. When fully staffed, there would be thirteen on the team, including the team leader. Team 1 was one of the largest teams.

During the six months I worked at SIA, we never had a "group" meeting involving all four teams. However, the four team leaders met with the group leader every morning and all the group leaders met with the car manager every afternoon. The only direct connection that Team 1 experienced with the other teams in our group was on the line. If one team was short several workers, the group leader would pull a worker from one of the other teams to assist that team.

Team 1 is located at one end of Trim; at the other end is an area called the U-turn. Here the cars literally make a U-turn. They are lifted up to about twenty feet and brought around to face in the opposite direction, ready to be lowered into the chassis area.

Some observations about the human component of the work setting at Trim and Final are in order before I describe the work itself. Concerning the sexual division of labor at SIA, men dominated the authority structure. Women accounted for only five out of the twenty-nine team leaders in Trim and Final, and none of the group leaders. Most of the women in production were located in Trim and Final, the lowest skilled and most labor-intensive area of the plant. Only three women held positions in the highest paying production jobs located in the Maintenance department. The three were all highly skilled millwrights from a local factory.

Selections from my field notes reflect the sexual division of labor, the ways in which that division was maintained, and the impact that it held for women at SIA:

> "On the way to work Joan told me about the problems she
> has had with her team leader. He came right out and told her
> that he did not want any women working under him. . . . She
> said that Mary (her teammate) has carpel tunnel and he
> makes fun of her for having it. Joan said that no matter how
> bad her hands ever hurt, she will not go to the doctor because
> of him. (October 24, 1989)

During down time, when the line was not moving, Team 1 performed tasks such as cleaning the area, fixing parts, and kaizening racks (designing and building racks to hold our parts). As the following excerpt indicates, despite the egalitarian ethic promoted by the company, a sexual division of labor emerges:

> Karen brought up today how our team leader assigns all the work according to sex. Karen and I always do the sweeping and the guys always kaizen. Karen and I make signs and repair wiring harnesses unless we can rope some of the guys into helping us. (November 3, 1989)

A woman from the final line experienced sexual discrimination which, if allowed to go unchecked, would have prevented her from ever advancing within the company. The following conversation took place during down time while we were hiding in a room containing personal computers, trying to look busy and stay out of the way so that we did not get work assignments that we disliked, such as sweeping and mopping the floor:

> Teresa (from the final line) told Randa, Karen (both from Team 1), Mindy (Team 2), and me about her evaluation by her team leader. (Anyone who wants to be a team leader has to have one of these evaluations.) Teresa said that she was devastated afterwards. He ranked her unacceptable on ability to train, oral communication and one other thing. When she asked him for an explanation, he said that he had never seen her train anyone nor speak before a group. She told us that she also had to do a self-evaluation and she told him that she had ranked herself very high in those two categories because she was formerly a music teacher and spoke in front of groups and trained people all day long. Her team leader then said that she had never worked any of the other stations, so she was not qualified to be a team leader because you have to master your entire area. Teresa said that the reason she hasn't is because he will not let her rotate. (She is the only woman on the team.) He also told her at the evaluation that she simply did not have the physical ability to perform any of the other stations. She will never qualify for team leader unless she can cross-train. (January 5, 1990)

With our encouragement, Teresa discussed this problem with her group leader. The group leader talked with her team leader and she was allowed to participate in team leader training. The following is another example of how the sexual division of labor was maintained:

> Teresa told us that when the company tried to move another woman down to their team right before Christmas, her team leader threw a fit. He was going to have to put the woman on the last station driving the cars off the line because the woman was in wrist splints and the group leader thought she could do that job. The team leader said that that was the station he used to reward the men during rotation, and another woman would prevent the men from receiving this reward. The group leader put the other woman back on her original team.
> (January 5, 1990)

Concerning racial division of labor, there were no blacks in positions of authority above team leader. I was aware of only one black man attaining the position of team leader in Trim and Final. He was in charge of one of the door lines in our group. In general, it seemed that very few blacks worked at SIA. The month after I started work at SIA, I counted ten blacks at a meeting of all Trim and Final Associates, about 150 people. Later one of the black workers in Materials was stymied in his attempt to advance within the company because his team leader would not give permission for him to attend team leader training classes after work. Team 1 members felt that he was a victim of racial discrimination:

> John told me today that Frank—the forklift driver who services my side of the line—asked him if we were satisfied with his work. John told him that of course we were and asked him why he wanted to know. Frank (who is black) said that his group leader refused to sign off for him so he could take the team leader training course (this was necessary in order to enter the pool of applicants for team leader). . . . I told the other members of the team about it. . . . Everyone is upset and says it's unfair. John said that Frank could file a grievance if there was a union. (November 16, 1989)

On July 22, 1993, the local newspaper reported that SIA was being sued for racial discrimination by a worker who claimed that he was fired because he is black and that the company maintains an atmosphere hostile to African Americans. The possibility of grounds for such conditions in transplants is evident in research on these operations. For example, there have been suggestions in the literature on the Japanese model that it uses site location to avoid hiring African Americans (Cole and Deskins 1988) and that "the screening procedures are discriminatory not only against unions, but also minorities, and perhaps older workers and women as well" (International Metalworkers Federation 1992:27).

A Typical Day

A typical day at SIA began at 6:25 A.M. (five minutes before the scheduled start of work) when music played over the loudspeaker, signaling morning exercises. Team members would line up and the team leader would lead us in our daily exercise routine. Team members had varied reactions to the exercises. Our team leader and one team member consistently seemed enthusiastic about the exercises; however, for the rest of us and for others in Trim and Final it was a different story. During my first day in the shop, there was a department meeting with the Trim and Final manager. At the end of the meeting questions were taken from the workers. The following field note entries illuminate how the workers felt about exercising:

> A woman asked: "What about the exercise policy, do we get
> slapped on the wrist for being late for exercises, or are we
> early for work?"
> The manager's response: "We encourage everyone to
> exercise."
> The woman: "Our team leader said he wanted to see
> everybody there."
> The manager: "They are not mandatory. That's why they are
> before the shift. But I'm not going to tell you not to do them."
> At this point, one of my teammates whispered to the rest of
> us: "Now she's ready for her team leader, she's got the
> manager's word." (July 31, 1989)

> Today was the first morning after the Trim and Final meeting.
> . . . This morning I noticed, and Terry mentioned it to me
> later, that there were fewer people exercising and several
> people entered the plant while we were performing ours
> (anyone entering the plant through the main door goes past

our station). The team we face while doing ours was nonexistent. Dave (teammate) said that even though our group leader had never said that they had to be there, they did feel a general pressure even though it is on their own time. (August 4, 1989)

The inspection team that exercised on the other side of final line has totally stopped. (August 10, 1989)

The team leader left Terry in charge today so no one exercised this morning, except Reese; he did it because he said it makes him feel better. The rest of us sat at the picnic table drinking coffee watching him. (November 10, 1989)

The first time I exercised I remember feeling embarrassed. It seemed juvenile. However, as time went on I began to feel differently about stretching out. Once the line was moving continually, I knew how easy it was to pull a muscle; so unless we refused as a team, to protest something, I exercised. The Japanese trainer usually joined us when we exercised; however, he was often late because the head trainer held meetings prior to work. About thirty seconds or so after exercises, the buzzer sounded to signal the beginning of our shift. The team did not wait for the buzzer. Instead, we formed a circle and began the morning team meeting. (According to the follow-up interviews in 1994, no one exercised by then. The music still plays, but workers no longer exercise.)

When official production was under way, the morning team meeting lasted only five minutes and team members found that they had little to say. During August and even into September, we generally had more time for meetings. Team members would bring up problems and suggestions. They complained, however, that their suggestions were seldom acted upon. Several times team members brought up their desire to rotate and to vote. Requests were acknowledged but simply ignored. Team members resented this. Once the line was moving continuously, team members also expressed resentment at even the brief time (five minutes) scheduled for the meetings because it interfered with their ability to get their stations set up for the day. The line began moving exactly at 6:35 A.M. whether our stations were ready or not.

At the end of those meetings the team performed a daily ritual. Team members would huddle in a manner similar to that of a sports team before a game. During the huddle, each person extended his or her left arm into the center of the circle, hands clenched into fists. The team leader then called on one member to deliver an inspirational message to the team. The usual message was, "Let's have a safe and productive day." A few team members sometimes told good-natured jokes, making light of the ritual. For the most part, it was embarrassing to be called upon and the jokes were a way for us to insert some control over the process. For example, during my last week in the plant the following occurred:

> This morning Tony gave the inspirational message for the group. He said: "This is Laurie's last week and working with her has been a pleasure. Let's build these cars for Laurie!" It was all a joke. Most of the messages are jokes. Terry will often give some Chinese proverb and then say some puffed up thing like—"I'm proud to be an American"—in a real deep voice. Everyone laughs. (January 8, 1990)

After the message, we all brought our right arms around into the circle with everyone's hands meeting in the center clenched into fists. While doing this, members shouted "Yosh!" and then broke up and went to work. Every team in the plant was instructed in performing this same ritual. It was our understanding that *yosh* was a cheer meaning something similar to "Let's go!"

At exactly 6:35 A.M. a buzzer sounded and the assembly line began to move. Unless someone pulled the cord and stopped the line, it ran until 8:30 A.M. when we took a ten-minute break. The line would screech to a halt and everyone in Trim and Final rested. Exactly ten minutes later the buzzer sounded and the line immediately began to move. There was no warning for team members to put on their aprons and gloves and walk back to their stations. Team members working the stations farthest from the break table were seen running back to the line.

At 10:30 A.M. the line stopped for a thirty-minute, unpaid lunch. Two or three team members often ate in the cafeteria with workers from their Orientation and Training classes. At 11:00 A.M. the line started up, again with no warning. At 1:00 P.M. the line stopped for another ten-minute break and at 3:00 P.M. the work day was over. Bathroom breaks were strongly discouraged when the line was moving. If you had to leave the line, you first had to get the team leader to take over your station. If the team leader was busy, you were out of luck. When there were no line stoppages it was a long and grueling day.

At one end of Team 1's area was a set of small lockers for personal items and opposite the lockers was a desk for the team leader (see figure

2). The lockers provided a kind of boundary between the line and a large picnic table where team members congregated during breaks. Every team had its own set of lockers and picnic table to provide a small break area. Nearly all of us spent breaks with our own team because ten minutes simply was not enough time to leave the immediate area. Team 1's break area was located right under the conveyer system bringing the cars to our team.

The noise in Trim and Final was constant and loud. Even during breaks, when the conveyers stopped, there was noise. Inevitably, during break time, contract employees would work on maintenance projects. Almost everyone on Team 1 wore ear plugs provided by the company.

The type of work each team member preformed varied as to its physical demands, its potential for injury, the speed at which it could be performed, and whether or not the team member could readily speak to others. For the most part, however, working on the line required our undivided attention. During plant start-up, workers had time for conversations between cars and even while working the stations. During our first few months, before line speed picked up, Team 1 played a guessing game while working on the line. One of us would think of a famous person and the rest of the team tried to figure out who it was within ten questions. (We made certain to stop playing when management came around). As line speed increased, time for interactions between workers and for periods of rest continually decreased. Not only were we more isolated as we were unable to interact; increased line speed was also accompanied by the emergence of injuries. At one point seven of the twelve members of Team 1 suffered from hand or wrist injuries. Once the speedup began, workers experienced constant pressure from the assembly line. Everyone was forced to work at a continuous, rapid pace.

Steps in Assembling a Car

Feeding Trim and Final were three other departments directly involved in building the cars and trucks at SIA: Stamping, Body, and Paint. The cars and trucks begin as blanks cut from a roll of steel. These crude pieces eventually form the bodies of the vehicles as they are stamped out in one of three enormous transfer presses. Each piece is mechanically transferred through a series of dies where the body parts are bent and refined with each pressing until they are ready to be taken to Body assembly and welded to other parts.

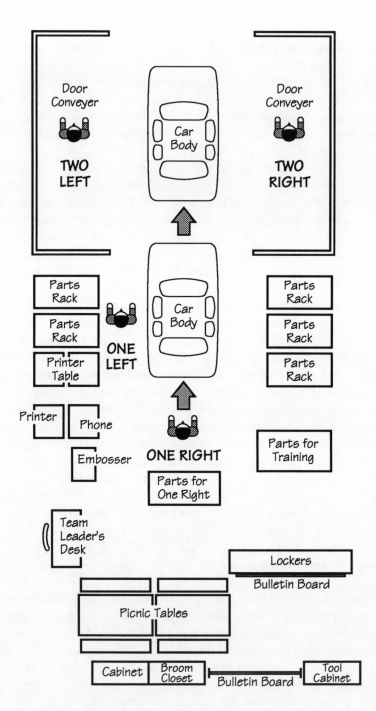

Figure 2. Break area and beginning work area for Team 1

The Stamping department is highly mechanized. I was told by a group leader that less than fifty people stamped out all of the necessary parts for the car and truck bodies. That worker, who had been in our training class and had previously worked in a stamping department, said that the mechanism that transfers the parts from one die to the next eliminates about twenty jobs. This was in comparison to the stamping plant where he had worked, where the parts were transferred by hand.

From Stamping, the parts are stacked up and taken to Body where more than 150 robots operate continuously. Most of the robots perform subassemblies, completing a task begun by a worker. For example, a worker might perform the initial welds on a subassembly, then place the part on a rack and send it inside a "cage" to the robot. The robot then bends over, thrusts two prongs into the part, rotates away from the worker and quickly turns the part at different angles as two giant "fingers" pinch both sides of the part, firing a spot weld at each movement. When finished, the part is dropped into a basket and the robot turns back and bends over to pick up the next subassembly. The robots perform thousands of welds. Sometimes the welds ignited sparks which flew as far as thirty feet out into the room. During my job interview at SIA, one of the team leaders described what it was like to work around the robots: "Sometimes a spark will get down inside of your shirt and you have to do a little dance 'til it's out."

The welded bodies are attached to the initial assembly line where the doors are hung and small items such as brackets are bolted to them. Each body is assigned a computer number for the conveyer system and given a token card. When a car or truck enters Trim and Final, the token card is dropped into a token card reader and information such as the model type, the wiring specifications, color, and other options are printed out on a specification and broadcast sheet. These sheets are attached to each vehicle to alert assembly line workers to the options for that particular vehicle. Once the token card has been hung on the body, the vehicle is placed in an overhead holding area until the conveyer system is ready to take it to Paint.

Most workers never went inside the Paint department. The potential for explosion is so great that it is surrounded by double concrete walls. Workers in Paint receive additional pay (about five cents an hour) for the hazardous work. The main reason that the rest of us were not allowed inside was not safety; it was to prevent dust from getting into the paint. Paint workers wore special polyester coveralls, which they found to be extremely warm. The coveralls controlled airborne fibers. Before entering the paint booth, workers passed through a room where they were dusted off with gusts of air.

When the cars and trucks are finished in Paint, they are held in one of the overhead conveyer systems. Six or seven at a time would move overhead and cross the room until they were above the truck final line, directly to the east of Team 1. While Team 1 members worked on the line, we would glance up and watch the cars as they joined the overhead lineup. At times there would be no cars in sight and just when team members were hoping for a break in the action, another car would appear around the corner and jerk into place. When the car body was directly in front of our line, but still about twenty feet in the air, it was switched by computer from the Paint conveyer to one of our gondola-like conveyers and the car would begin its steady descent into Team 1's area. Once on Trim and Final's conveyer system, the bodies were spaced about three or four feet apart.

The car and truck sides operate basically the same except for a few physical differences in the vehicles and the conveyer systems. Trucks are built with a frame and the cars are uni-bodies, so the car side does not attach the body to a frame. Also, workers on the car side remove the doors and send them to a separate line to be assembled. The truck side assembles the doors while these are still attached to the bodies. There are also physical differences in the conveyer systems. Trucks rest on post-like stands protruding about a foot and a half from the floor. The conveyer is in the floor at the very center of the line, so that the moving part of the floor does not extend beyond the sides of the truck. Thus the trucks remain at the same height throughout most of assembly process, making it necessary for workers in the chassis and final areas to stand in pits underneath the trucks as they work. (It is my understanding that older U.S. plants have pits but that they are currently being eliminated in most plants.)

On the car side, there are no pits. The cars move by means of an overhead conveyer system. The carriers, referred to as hangers, resemble giant gondolas with four large, bright orange arms. The arms curve around the sides of each car, holding it up from the bottom. Since the conveyer is overhead, the height of the car can be changed as it enters different areas. Hence people working on the chassis do not have to work in a pit to attach the rear end and do the underbody work. However, even though they do not have to work in a pit, depending on how tall they are, they work all day either with their arms extended above their heads or with their heads bent at a sharp angle.

When the car enters the chassis work area, it is lifted to about five feet above the floor. The engine is thrust up into the car by means of a jig and workers attach it as they stand underneath the car. In chassis, large items, such as the rear end and the engine, are subassembled and mounted on jigs. The line is then stopped as the team bolts these large subassemblies into place with giant impact wrenches. Chassis is the only area where the car stops. In every other area, the cars continue to move while people work. The line is designed so that the chassis stops do not affect the flow of vehicles. Only if the chassis workers are unable to install the part within takt time is the rest of the line affected.

Takt time is the cycle time, or the length of time that each worker is given to complete his or her job. Everyone on the line and in the entire plant operated under the same takt time. Each team was divided into separate work stations with one person responsible for completing the tasks assigned to that station. Except for chassis, where the line stopped, takt time is also related to distance, as each station is given a prescribed distance to work on the car. The speed of the line determines the amount of time each worker has to complete the tasks of a station. It was common knowledge that once SIA was fully staffed and trained, takt time would be three minutes and forty seconds. When I left SIA, the line was down to about a five-minute takt time.

Following chassis are two teams on the final line. Even though it was called the final line, it was not a separate line but was directly connected to chassis. The car entered the final line resting on its tires so the overhead conveyer was removed. Once the tires are put on the car, the gondola-like hanger automatically spreads apart and rises up and into the overhead conveyer system, where it lines up to receive another body from Paint. At this point, the floor under the wheels of the car becomes the conveyer and moves it along.

In Final, things such as carpeting and seats are installed. Final also injects all of the liquids into the engine, the battery is installed, doors are reattached, the steering wheel is attached, an on-line inspection is performed, some gasoline is put into the car, and the car is started and driven off the line.

Final is responsible for the last formal inspection on the assembly line. In addition to this inspection, there are inspections at two other places referred to as "check-man" points, one in trim and one in chassis. If any defect is discovered on the line, the team responsible is notified by telephone and the team leader must see that the problem is fixed. In addition to these formal checking stations, all workers are expected constantly to check their own work and the work of the other team members.

As many repairs as humanly possible are made right on the line. This was often a difficult job because the car continued to move and another team might be working on it. Repairs were necessary for several reasons: a part might be forgotten, a plug could be improperly seated, an item that required a torque check might not have been marked, or the body might have some type of damage, such as a scratch in the paint. All of these items are subject to repair while on the line.

The reason SIA pushed team members to do on-line repair was so that the cars could pass inspection in the final area without having to be diverted to the repair line or to paint touch-up. When the cars passed the on-line inspection, they were called "direct runners." SIA's goal was one hundred percent direct runners without any line stoppages. Team members voiced suspicions that management was receiving bonuses tied to the number of direct runners.

At times, the extremes that the car side went to in order to tag a car a direct runner were seen by team members as ridiculous. For example, when we were building the first car for the official start of production, there was tremendous pressure to make it a direct runner. As luck would have it, there were several problems with that particular vehicle. At one point, even the windshield had to be replaced when it was discovered that the date on that particular batch of sealant had expired. Technically, however, that car was a direct runner. This was managed by continually stopping the line. At one point, the car was actually pushed off to the side of the line while repairs were made. Then it was pushed back on so that it could be driven off the end as a direct runner. Of course, when official production began, the line would not be stopped for such continuous and frivolous repairs. Production quotas prevailed.

If a car did not require any additional repair or paint touch-up, it was driven from the final line to a separate inspection line. Here it was tested for things such as water leaks and body damage and all safety items were double-checked. A final undercoating was applied and, if there were no repairs, the car was driven to a staging area, ready to go.

Team 1 Tasks

A Japanese trainer organized Team 1 so that each person stayed on one side of the car working opposite another team member. There was one exception. "One right" finished that station before "one left" began working and each worked both sides of the car. Some of the parts were installed by two people, working across from each other, but most were installed by only one person. Each person was responsible for maintaining his or her own station. Responsibilities included making certain there were enough parts to get through the day, that the racks holding the parts were in good condition, that everything was arranged in the most efficient manner, that the area was kept clean, and that all tools were put into a locked cabinet at the end of the shift.

Keeping parts stocked was often very stressful. SIA uses "just-in-time" production, a method that puts the burden of parts shortages on the shoulders of line workers and material handlers. Each material handler is in charge of stocking all of the parts for approximately three teams along one side of the line. This involves hundreds of parts. Every morning Materials (as team members referred to the people who delivered the parts to the line) attempted to get enough parts on the racks to last us through the day. However, the racks were not large enough to hold a full day's supply of the larger parts and some parts came in different options, so it was difficult to keep enough variety on hand. With just-in-time production, parts are not kept stockpiled in storage areas but are delivered just in time. Too often, this was literally true. Almost daily, some member of the team would experience the pressure of an impending parts shortage as Materials searched for the part on a truck at the loading dock. Many times, Materials would be ripping open a box of parts as the car missing that part was leaving the station concerned. The part did not arrive just in time and the vehicle would continue to move down the line without it. The line was not allowed to be stopped until it became absolutely necessary for that part to be in place before installation of the next began. When this happened, the team leader and anyone else who knew the installation would scramble down the line installing the part in the cars that had been skipped. There was tremendous pressure on team leaders never to let the line stop as each team was credited with down time.

The normal procedure for notifying Materials of potential parts shortages began in the morning at the beginning of the shift. Each team member would notify the team leader as to how soon parts would be required and the team leader would telephone Materials if quick action was necessary. More than once, team members found themselves running flat-out down the line in search of the material handler to warn that they were dangerously low on a part. While a team member was away from the line it continued to move, so that upon returning, the line worker would not only be about to run out of a part but would also be behind on everything!

Falling behind was something everyone tried to avoid at all costs. This was not so much because we were concerned about productivity but for a far more personal reason: falling behind on the line was a miserable experience. It made work chaotic and drastically increased the pressure and stress of the job. Under nondisruptive conditions, it was a matter of pride for a team member to complete his or her share of the work. If a materials problem arose, however, there was no stigma attached to falling behind. In the case of shortages, the pressure was from above, not from other team members; however, with just-in-time production the team was always on the verge of falling behind.

In addition to the duties directly related to working on the line, team members were responsible for keeping their stations neat and clean; keeping daily records on the level of the oilers, the air line pressure, and each car number; and keeping tools in good condition. When it came to housekeeping, team members were pretty lax. The group leader was constantly haranguing the team and giving us bad check marks for "dust bunnies" under the racks, but this had little effect. Team members simply did not care and cleanup was one job all of us hated. Unless we were given a direct order, housekeeping was generally ignored. Management was constantly trying to get the team to use down time (unscheduled line stops) for housekeeping. However, members of Team 1 considered line stoppages free time and were reluctant to give it up. When line stops occurred, team members could be seen either standing around visiting or, if someone was behind, using part of the time to get caught up.

Line stops occurred for several reasons. Usually, however, it was because someone pulled the red cord. Every station had a yellow cord and a red cord hanging above the line. The cords were attached to red and yellow lights located above each work station. When a worker pulled either cord, one of the lights would come on. A team member who was having difficulty and anticipated failing to meet takt time would pull the yellow cord, which did not stop the line. Instead, it triggered the computer system and the team's music would be played throughout the department over the sound system. (Each team was assigned a few bars of music.) When anyone on the car or truck side pulled the red or yellow cord, the music for that team was played over and over and over again, and the light above that person's station remained on until some action was taken.

When the yellow cord was pulled, it was the duty of the team leader to get to the troubled station within a few seconds before the line automatically stopped. The station concerned was easy to find due to the bright yellow light. Once there, the team leader immediately pulled the cord a second time to stop the music, turn off the light, and prevent the line from stopping. The team leader then attempted to handle the problem. If unable to fix it, he or she could pull the red cord. This was quite unlike what we were told in orientation and training (that anyone could stop the line—especially for quality reasons), unless there is a safety emergency, only team leaders or higher ranking company officials have authority to pull the red cord and stop the line. When the red cord is pulled, the line stops, the red light above that team member's station lights up, and the team's music comes back on and plays until the line starts up again.

Since the same few bars of music play continuously during a line stop, there were many complaints by team members that the music drove them crazy. Some days our team leader was constantly answering the yellow cord. Other days no one pulled it.

On the line, the team member responsible for each station had the car under his or her control for a predetermined distance. Team members walked next to the bodies, installing parts, as the vehicles continued their procession down the line. The distance did not vary. However, the speed of the line could be changed so that the amount of time team members had to work on the car could be increased or decreased. Although takt time did not vary from station to station, many of the processes did not work as smoothly as anticipated by Team 1's Japanese trainer, so some stations took more time than others. One reason for this was that people simply do not work comfortably at the same speed; some team members could just barely keep up.

All of the stations on our team were designed by Team 1's first Japanese trainer. He used a book which told exactly how many seconds (to the tenth of a second) it should take to install every single part, even the smallest plug. Procedures were broken down by steps, from which he calculated how many parts each station could install within a takt time of three minutes, forty seconds. He then determined the number of stations it would take Team 1 to install all of the parts assigned to us. Our trainer claimed that he had designed each station so that we would have several seconds left after finishing our jobs. He jokingly told us, we could each "have an armchair" at our stations for resting between cars. He believed we would have plenty of time for the tasks of our stations once we had a full crew. At the slowed speed, many team members were doing one station and part of a second station; it was a hectic pace for some and a reasonable pace for others.

"One right" was the first station to work on the body (team members called vehicles "bodies"). This station was right next to the break area and the other stations followed (see figure 2). While the car was still at least eight or nine feet above the floor, one right would stand on a platform and begin inserting about twenty rubber plugs into the underside of the car. The plugs were somewhat difficult to insert because they were baffled and the undercoating on the bottom of the car often clogged up some of the holes. When that happened, one right would open up the holes with a screwdriver. This cut into takt time and increased the pressure of the team member's job. After the plugs were inserted and the car had descended, one right attached the torsion bars to the trunk lid and applied the clear protection strips to the rear fenders.

One left was the station with which I became most familiar as it was the last station I was assigned. The following is a step-by-step account of that process (these directions are not from the standard Operation Instruction Sheet. I wrote these in my notes after my last day at work):

1. Go to the car and take the token card off a wire on the front of the car.
2. Pick up the 2 VIN (vehicle identification number) plates from the embosser and check the plates to see that they have the same number.
3. Insert the token card into the token card reader.
4. While waiting for the computer output, break down the key kit for the car by pulling the 3 lock cylinders and the lock code from the bag.
5. Copy the vehicle control number and color number onto the appearance check sheet.
6. Inspect the car for damage sustained while in the Paint department. Look over the outside of the car and open each door and inspect all areas that are not later covered. Mark down any scratches, chips, dents, or any other damage on a sketch of the car located on the appearance check sheet.
7. Go to a rack and pick up a hood stay, the work basket containing plugs and grease, the hood jig, and lay them in the engine compartment.

8. Lift the hood and put the hood jig in place so it will hold the hood open while installing the hood stay.

9. Insert the rubber hood stay grommet.

10. Insert the hood stay into the grommet, lift the hood, and prop it open with the hood stay. Insert a rubber hose at the top of the hood stay to insure that the hood will not fall while people work in the engine compartment.

11. Go to the printer and get the broadcast sheet. Check the VIN numbers on the sheet against the plates and check to see that the plates match the coding for front or four-wheel drive.

12. Attach the broadcast sheet to the front edge of the hood with masking tape.

13. Check the VIN number from the broadcast sheet to the number engraved on the car body at the back of the engine compartment.

14. From your basket, pick up two rubber hood buffers and slide them onto the two hooks on either side of the engine compartment so that the hood will rest on them when closed.

15. Pick up a right-side fender cover from the right side of the line and attach it over the right fender.

16. Pick up 2 screw grommets and the fender top grommet from the basket and insert them in the proper holes under the left front fender.

17. Attach the front left fender cover (located on the left side of the line) and remove the hood jig and the basket from the car.

18. Tear off the specification sheet from second printer, attach it to the clipboard with the appearance sheet, and put the key lock code on the specification sheet.

19. Carry the clipboard, the trunk lock cylinder, token card, and small black VIN plate to the car, put everything except the clipboard in the box on the car carrier and insert the clipboard into the slot underneath the car on the carrier.

20. Get the riveter, the two door lock cylinders, pick up 2 rivets and the large VIN plate. Carry them to the car.

21. Toss the yellow cylinder to the passenger side and lay the white cylinder on the floor of the driver's side.

22. Rivet the large VIN plate to the left-hand center pillar.
23. Begin with step one on the next car.

Before one left finished, two left and two right would often begin working. Whenever possible, all of us tried to work ahead by beginning our station tasks before the car actually crossed the line to enter our areas. This gave team members an edge against breakdowns and parts shortages, things that caused us to fall behind. Anyone on the team who noticed that another team member needed help would usually pitch in and help; however, it was a matter of pride to be able to keep one's station under control.

In U.S. auto plants, working ahead or speeding up for a time has been a method for breaking monotony and giving workers some control over the regulation of their work. At SIA workers naturally attempted to do the same; but when I interviewed workers in February 1994, each reported that there was absolutely no chance to work ahead and create any spare time or relieve the tension. The line was simply too fast.

The operations performed by two left and two right were nearly identical. One very small element in their set of tasks became the focus of the entire team. Both stations were responsible for inserting small rigid plastic plugs into the sides of the doors before doors were removed. Two plugs were inserted in the front and two in the back door. Team members had been trained to push the two plugs into the holes simultaneously, using both thumbs. The force that was exerted on the thumbs resulted in pain and inflammation involving the tendons that lead from wrist to thumb, so team members unofficially kaizened the process to devise a method for preventing injury. I refer to this as an unofficial kaizen because it was done independently of management. We decided what was needed to make the process safer and then one of us made the tool we designed.

The reason we did not get the team leader or group leader directly involved was because it took so long. Resolution probably would have taken months. When team or group leaders told us to kaizen something, they would discuss our suggestions among themselves and then they would make the final decision, often involving none of our suggestions. Sometimes, it seemed as though they already knew what they wanted before we kaizened. It was almost as though we were simply going through the motions. If you wanted something done quickly, you did it without their knowledge. In this case, the solution was to use a short metal rod for pushing in the plugs. However, as with so many of the protective innovations that team members came up with, there was a down side. These altered processes usually took more time and no adjustment was made in the amount of work those workers had to accomplish within takt time.

Three left installed the wiring for the ceiling spot lamp and attached the left seat belt to the body. Tension on the seat belt bolts was safety-checked with a torque wrench. After three left installed the seat belt, the fuel pipe was clipped into place and the height control plug inserted into a hole in the front side of the car. This was a very difficult plug to insert, so that team member soaked it in soapy water. It made insertion easier, although it meant that that team member's fingers were wet with soapy water most of the day.

The last task for three left was to work with three right to install the toeboard insulator, a difficult process because the toeboard was heavy and unwieldy and usually did not line up the way it was supposed to. The result was that three left and three right strained their hands and wrists tugging and pushing it into place. Three right's process was very similar to that of three left. Installing the other front seat belt, ceiling room lamp wiring, brake pipe, and finally, the toeboard insulator.

Four right was never able to work ahead because that process involved climbing up and inside the car body after toeboard installation was completed. Four right would sling the bulkhead harness (containing all the wiring for the dashboard, fuse box, and part of the engine compartment) over his or her shoulder, grab a blower unit in one hand, a radio antenna and work basket in the other hand, and proceed to the car body. The bulkhead was an enormous wiring harness, twelve to fourteen feet long with several cables of different lengths attached to it. Before climbing into the car, four right inserted the main grommet into the front right pillar and the front pillar insulator. Once inside the car body, four right's concentration turned to the bulkhead harness. Three cables with large connectors dangling from the ends had to be fed into the engine compartment through a hole in the dash. The hole was just barely large enough, so that the intensity of the physical force applied by four right's hands was dramatically increased once working to maneuver the final cable through the hole. Next the blower unit was attached with an impact wrench, the bit on the wrench then being changed in order to attach the car antenna. The antenna was a trouble spot. The bolt on the body was often not properly crimped and the antenna screw broke off in the hole. When this occurred, four right would fall hopelessly behind.

While four right worked inside the car, four left would be installing the front left wiring harness. Installation of this harness required that team member to work on his or her knees, up under the left front fender. One team member kaizened the station and designed a stool on wheels for four left to sit on while working under the fender.

Four left and four right were considered the most physically demanding of all the stations. When installing the front left wiring harness, four left expended a great deal of energy tugging and twisting it into place. Four right was forced to climb up into every car to install the bulkhead harness. Both of the workers assigned to those stations suffered wrist injuries.

Five left installed the trunk pull cable, gas cover cable, and fuse box bracket. Five left also finished part of the installation of the front left wiring harness; attached the trunk and gas cover cables with an impact wrench; attached the ground wire for the front left wiring harness; finished snapping the harness to the body; and before leaving the car, five left bolted the fuse box bracket onto the left front pillar. The chronically troublesome spot for five left was attaching the ground wire, which often required use of a regular screw driver to get it tightened down. This took extra time and was also a strain on the wrist.

Five right installed the rear wiring harness, extending along the inside of the passenger side of the car. Although installing this harness was fairly uncomplicated, it was known as a "thumb killer." One of the clips that had to be pushed into the body required forcing with one's thumbs. When combined with the difficult clip, even the easy ones took their toll. Team members attempted to design a tool for inserting the difficult clip but nothing was satisfactory. Most of the people who worked that station for any length of time experienced some level of injury to their thumbs.

Six right worked in the engine compartment. This station was responsible for installing the wiper motor, hood latch and cable, and the resonator. To do this, six right had to crawl on hands and knees under the front of the car. Clipping the hood cable into place was another job that often led to injury to the thumb and finger tendons. Attaching the wiper motor to the rear of the engine compartment required an impact wrench with a twelve-inch extension. Such a long extension created excessive vibration. One team member said that she "could feel it clear through to her elbows."

While six right worked in the engine compartment, six left attached the bulkhead harness to more than twenty electrical connections. Reaching these connections required bending the right hand at sharp angles while pushing connectors together. The combination of the bending and pushing caused wrist injury. Six left was also in wrist splints when I left SIA.

Shop Floor Reality vs. Company Philosophy

The *SIA Associate Handbook* had told us "We are a company that places great importance on respect for people, commitment to safety, and quality in everything we do. These three are essential to our success. *People, safety,* and *quality* are the watchwords that dominate our workday" (1989:7).

The issue of stopping the line and who had the authority to pull the red cord was one of several inconsistencies between the company's egalitarian philosophy and our experience on the shop floor. In Orientation and Training, we had been told that "everyone is an Associate at SIA, from the company president on down." Team members, however, felt that the term *Associate* was used to designate those of us who worked on the line or in support areas like material handling, not for management. When addressing team members, management would often begin statements with the phrase, "We are all Associates here at SIA." Even though team members used terms like *team leader* or *group leader* to refer to people in those positions, they never referred to each other or other line workers as Associates. Workers referred to each other by name, team, or department. Managers and group leaders used Associate when referring to workers collectively, and often as individuals. Sometimes it was even used to refer to one of us in the third person, while we were present. For example, once while the car manager was talking to my group leader and me, he turned to the group leader and said: "Well, it looks like the Associate is doing her job," speaking as though I was not present.

The term *Associate* was one way of distinguishing workers directly employed by SIA from contract workers. Contract workers did everything from maintaining the conveyer systems, cleaning the locker rooms and office area, running the cafeteria, and working in security to keeping up the grounds. Some of them even held clerical positions. For the most part, there was no interaction between these contract workers and Associates. (Contract workers are not the same as the temporary workers SIA widely employs today. Temporaries work on the line with regular team workers. I discovered through interviews during February 1994 that up to half of some teams are temporary workers. Temporaries are hired through a local agency and it was reported by Associates that they receive about ten dollars per hour. SIA pays them no benefits.)

But the overriding discrepancy between shop floor reality and company philosophy involved injuries. Immediately after official start of production (SOP), there was an outbreak of hand and wrist injuries. Since Team 1 was located at one end of the plant, anyone using the bathrooms on that side of the building had to walk past us. Because of our location and the easily identified method of treatment for hand and wrist injuries, we could observe the dramatic increase. Within only a few weeks, dozens of workers were wearing splints on their wrists and foreams. People continued to work, but their wrists were immobilized in splints. According to several injured workers, the company physician had either diagnosed them with carpal tunnel syndrome or, more typically, told them they were showing symptoms of it and their diagnosis was "overwork syndrome." At first, no one was taken off the line. Unless the company physician gave a direct order to remove an injured person from a station, each continued on the same job that had caused the injury.

The type of work we engaged in at SIA made us especially vulnerable to various repetitive-motion injuries, as was and is the case throughout the auto industry. Nationally, repetitive-motion injuries such as carpal tunnel syndrome increased 58 percent in 1989 over 1987 and workers in the automobile industry had an injury rate of 28.5 for every 100 full-time workers, more than three times the rate of all workplaces (*Labor Notes,* January 1990:4). At Mazda, the Fucinis found an alarming increase in worker injuries when the plant began approaching full production. Recordable injuries increased by 50 percent between June and September of 1988—a rate of 42.6 days lost for every 100 workers from June 1988 to May 1989—and injuries were considerably higher than in the Big Three auto plants in Michigan (1990:175).

At SIA we were living proof that the speedup, repetition, and physical stress of assembly line work was detrimental to our health. Berggren, Bjorkman, and Hollander's (1991) field trip to the Japanese transplants reported growing health and safety complaints due to the intense pace, repetitiveness, and long working hours. These conditions led to cumulative trauma disorders or repetitive strain injuries. At Mazda they found an unusually high incidence of carpal tunnel syndrome with the total number of work-related injuries at three times the level of that in comparable American plants (Berggren et al. 1991:55). When Berggren's team visited Honda in Anna, Ohio, management would not even admit that this was a problem in any way related to conditions of production. Instead, the company blamed the workers, stating: "There are weak and strong people. And there are right and wrong attitudes" (Berggren et al. 1991:55).

My field notes make reference to some of our injuries:

> I went to the (company) doctor this morning because my thumbs have been bothering me since we stepped up production—about a month now. He said I have tendonitis. He gave me wrist splints to wear at work, prescribed exercises for my hands, and told me not to push any more plugs on the cars for a week when he'll see me again. (November 22, 1989)

> Randa went to the doctor today. She has early signs of carpal tunnel. She is restricted from doing the toeboard insulator. . . . Half of Tom's team (Team 2) is down. Candy cannot do any kind of pinching motion or her hand goes immediately numb, and Tammy is on light duty. Ike is home with strep. (December 7, 1989)

> I saw Joan from the truck side in the bathroom this morning and she said that everyone on her team is now in splints (4 of them. . . . I know a lot of people in splints—the four on Joan's team, a woman right across from us on the truck finish line, two people on Tom's team, Karen, Randa, Mike and me. Plus there are many people I see with them on that I simply don't know, or don't know what team they are on. (December 11, 1989)

> Three of the men on our team have been to the doctor with wrist and thumb complaints, just as many as the women. (December 11, 1989)

> I talked to Debbie on the truck line from my training class. She has splints on both arms. . . . Debbie used to be a line supervisor at a factory. She said that she now understands what the women under her went through with their carpal tunnel. The doctor told her she has it in one hand and is symptomatic in the other. He is sending her to physical therapy. (December 14, 1989)

> Our team leader is going to go to the doctor tonight after work. She has been waking up all through the night with

carpal tunnel symptoms (numbness in her hands). . . . Terry
told me he is also going to go back to the doctor because his
wrists are still bothering him. There are now two men with
splints on from the door line. They are both big men. . . . Our
team leader has never taken Karen off her station (the station
where she sustained her wrist injury). (December 18, 1989)

Karen and Randa went in for checkups today; they are still in
splints and Mindy (another team member) went in for the first
time. Now she is also in splints. Randa told me that her friend
Carey on the truck finish line is probably going to get splints
also; her hands have been waking her up at night. . . . A third
person is now wearing them on the door line. . . . I asked
Steve from Team 2 how many people he thought were having
wrist problems. He said he would guess that easily 25% are
having problems, even if they haven't been put in splints.
(December 20, 1989)

Candy from Team 2 experienced some of the earliest and most severe
symptoms associated with hand injuries. She was one of the first to suffer
pain and numbness in her hands, which continued for several weeks before she finally saw the company doctor. During that time, she said that
she often complained to her team leader about pain and numbness, hoping that he would change her job or send her for medical help. Unfortu-
nately, she did not realize—as none of us did at that time—that we had
to ask to be seen by the doctor. No team leader that Team 1 members
were aware of ever directed an Associate with a wrist or hand complaint
to see the doctor without a specific request from the injured individual.
	Candy finally sought help after she noticed someone from Team 1 in
splints. Karen from Team 1 described to Candy how her hands were
"falling asleep" at night and causing her to wake up. Once awake, she
would shake them to get some feeling back. Finally, Karen saw a leaflet
the company had distributed to our team and posted on a bulletin board,
describing the symptoms associated with carpal tunnel syndrome. That
was when she sought help. Karen asked our team leader to refer her to
the company doctor and Candy followed her lead.
	Nearly everyone with early carpal tunnel symptoms was put into
splints and given anti-inflammatory medication. In addition, Candy wore
isotoner support gloves to help control the swelling. Her injuries pro-
gressed to the point that with almost any movement, her hands became

numb. Finally they began to fall asleep just hanging at her sides. Eventually, she had cortisone injected into each wrist and a few weeks later she was sent home on Worker's Compensation. She was called back a few times (once to the Paint department to inspect cars), but only on a temporary basis. After a few days in each job she would be sent home. Candy was afraid of losing her job but she was even more afraid of having permanently damaged her hands. No one seemed to be able to tell us what the long-term effects are from such injuries.

Debbie and Candy represented only a fraction of the workers who experienced hand and wrist injuries in Trim and Final. In our group alone, seven of twelve people on Team 1, three of nine from Team 2, and three people on the door line had such injuries. The man who took over Candy's station ended up in the same situation as hers: off work with hand injuries. All of these injuries occurred within a matter of weeks after SOP.

Needless to say, wrist injuries became a constant topic of conversation. Workers discussed them before work in the bathroom and on breaks, anxiously comparing notes on symptoms, diagnoses, and progress reports from the doctor. We discussed the pros and cons of the different types of splints and the exercises given for therapy. In addition to the injuries, the splints themselves were a cause of embarrassment and interfered with the normal routine of life outside of work. Getting them clean was a major concern. After being worn twenty-four hours a day, they smelled terrible. One woman said her husband was embarrassed to be seen in public with her while she wore splints—afraid people would think that he beat her. Another woman complained that the splints made it difficult to bathe her children, cook supper, or do any normal household chores.

Besides interfering with home life, splints also were an interference on the job. Some people even resorted to removing the splints at work because they slowed one down so much; people were afraid of not being able to keep up with the line. Others could not perform their jobs at all because their hands would no longer fit into tight places. Workers were afraid that their injuries would become more than an inconvenience and eventually progress into disabling conditions like Candy's. For her, it was not simply difficult or awkward to do household chores; she was physically unable to cook, sweep, or do even the most minor task. The greatest fear, however, was not knowing what the long-term effects might be. As one young team member said: "When I'm finally a grandmother I want to be able to pick up my grandkids and do things for them. No job is worth giving up that."

Although the company attempted to cut back on the injury rate, Team 1 members were not impressed with its approach. On the surface, it appeared that the company was doing everything possible, but team members believed that it was only treating the symptoms, not the cause. The doctor tried to stress prevention and worked with many of us on programs for strengthening our hands. The company began talking to new workers during their training classes, warning them of the possibilities of injury and encouraging them to exercise their wrists and hands. Eventually, an occupational therapist was brought in to work with the injured. We were not dissatisfied with the company's medical response to our injuries. It was prevention that was weak. Strengthening one's hands was obviously important but we knew that the underlying causes of injury were greater than what could be addressed by physical strength.

The company hired an ergonomist to observe our work. He observed many of the jobs which were repeatedly causing injuries to our team. However, Team 1 never experienced any tangible evidence that such observations actually led to substantial changes in the structure or timing of our jobs. For example, he observed us installing the bulkhead harness, making the wiring connections for the dash and fuse box, installing the toeboard insulator, and putting in the rear wiring harness. All of these jobs were known to cause injury but only one change was ever made to any of them while I was there and it was made by a Japanese trainer, not by the ergonomist.

The job that was changed was the installation of the toeboard insulator. The problem with the toeboard was that the vendor manufacturing the toeboard for SIA was at one extreme of the tolerance for placing the holes in the toeboard, while the body shop welding the stud bolts that the holes fit over was at the opposite extreme. This meant that the burden of fit fell on three right and three left, the workers doing the installation. When the fit was really bad, installing the toeboard required a tremendous amount of twisting and straining and it was necessary to bend one's wrists backward to a sharp, unnatural angle in order to do the job. While that team member worked, she said, she could feel her wrists tingle under the stress.

The change to the toeboard installation was made by our Japanese kaizen trainer. His solution was to hang a heat lamp over the toeboards, making them more pliable. The heat lamps helped but were not a sufficient remedy. As the pile of toeboards went down, the lamps were farther away and less effective. Those of us with experience on that job suggested that the company send back those toeboards and make the vendor concentrate on designing a toeboard that fit the car, instead of making a line worker force the part to fit. (That did not happen while I was there.) After Randa was injured on the toeboard, our group leader filled out the accident report with her. His immediate solution to the problem: "Put a stronger Associate on the job." Randa's response: "Pretty soon, that 'strong' Associate will be on 'his' knees."

A work change suggestion made by the ergonomist and the company doctor involved the door assembly on the truck line. As a preventive measure, they provided splints to everyone doing that job and told people to wear these while they worked. In theory they had the right approach but it was an impractical and impossible solution. People could not fit their hands inside the doors with the splints on! Even though the company seemed to have good intentions, the management approach to preventing injuries never penetrated the underlying causes. It tried to change people to fit the job, instead of making the job fit for people. Team members believed that line speedup, as well as repetition and stress, were the keys to the injury rate. As soon as the line began its steady speedup, the injury rate skyrocketed.

At first, a majority of workers with hand and wrist injuries seemed to be women; however, men soon experienced the same injuries. Nevertheless, since women appeared to be afflicted sooner and more often than men, a form of sexual harassment emerged which threatened to interfere further with safety. For example, in Paint, one of the men who operated a hand sprayer wore splints. Some of his male fellow workers in Paint said that he had "Corporal Klinger's disease," implying that the man was faking a woman's disease in order to get out of work. (A character from the movie and television program *MASH,* Corporal Klinger is a man who wears women's clothes in an attempt to be released from duty in the army.) Besides being stigmatizing, it was untrue. No one that any of us was aware of, aside from Candy, had ever been taken off the line because of having hands in splints and even she was not removed immediately. Faking carpal tunnel was not the road to an easier job.

Team 1's concern was that once carpal tunnel became a stigma, many men and women would be too embarrassed to seek help when their wrists were bothering them. In fact, it did take a great amount of encouragement from the rest of us before some of the injured men on Team 1 sought medical help, even though they were aware that they were experiencing symptoms associated with carpal tunnel. A woman from the truck line told me that her team leader made fun of another woman on the team because she had carpal tunnel. Her response was: "No matter how bad my hands hurt me, I will never go in to the doctor because of him." A woman from another team on the truck side had carpal tunnel in one wrist. She reported that her team leader told her: "The women at SIA are a bunch of weaklings and we should send them off to lift barbells for a few weeks."

In reality, both men and women were afflicted with hand and wrist injuries and eventually workers began to perceive this as a plant-wide problem. I asked one worker from Team 2 how widespread he thought the problem was. He believed that it was very widespread, stating: "I would guess that easily twenty-five percent [of the workforce] are having problems [with their wrists and hands]."

According to the company nurse, Trim and Final had by far the most hand complaints but she said these were increasing in other departments. While waiting for the doctor, sometimes we met people from other departments. One man from Body mentioned that he had been a welder for the last fifteen years. Since he came to SIA he developed what the doctor referred to as a "trigger finger." His hand was in a clenched position around his welding gun all day long and when he tried to open up his fingers, they did not move. While sitting in the doctor's office, he closed his fingers across his palm and then tried to open them; they jerked open about an inch and then closed up again. He was visibly shaken. Welding was his trade and he said he was worried that he had jeopardized it by coming to SIA.

During one of my visits to the company doctor, I talked to a man who worked in Body on the assembly line. His job was to hang doors on the trucks. He said that when he first started, the doors did not fit properly and he had to use all the strength he could muster to push doors up and against each body to get the hinges to fit. He had pulled many of the muscles around his chest, which left him feeling weak all over. His main concern, however, was that his hands went numb after he fell asleep at night and this woke him up. He was not getting any sleep.

When I talked to the doctor, he seemed convinced that, for the most part, the injuries occurred because we were lacking in strength. During one examination I asked him if men got carpal tunnel as well as women, or if it was a "woman's disease." He assured me that there were plenty of men out there who were "out of shape" and not used to working at a physically demanding job.

One can understand how a lack of strength could contribute to injury; however, in many cases the injuries could be attributed to more specific conditions associated with the work process rather than to a worker's physical capacity. Consistently working with poorly fitting parts or working with wrists bent at unnatural angles created problems for workers' health regardless of their strength. Another common problem on both the car and truck sides was having to use one's thumbs to push plugs and clips into the vehicle bodies. In addition, there was the constant repetition, which seemed especially damaging when it involved small hand movements such as fitting nuts onto bolts with one's fingers.

At one point our Japanese trainer brought to work some "Japanese medicine" for our hands. Terry and I decided to try it during morning break. The trainer unwrapped a box of what appeared to be small cone-shaped incense candles. He placed them at certain points on our wrists and lit them with a match. We were told to leave them on while they heated up. He told us that these were what workers used in Japan to relieve their pains. They did not work for us, but then neither did aspirin after a while.

No matter how concerned about safety the company claimed to be, Team 1 could see no substantial improvement forthcoming. Jobs were not restructured or retimed and safety was our responsibility instead of the company's. SIA was unable to provide us with a "safe" workplace. It was not unsafe as regards common hazards, things that cause accidents and can easily be fixed; it was unsafe because of the work process itself. The repetition and speed of assembly line work was inherently harmful to workers. Any solutions that would reduce the work intensity created by repetition and line speed would threaten production quotas—something team members believed the company would never consider. Instead, we were left to our own devices of cobbling together makeshift tools and turning to each other for help. SIA might claim to be different from other companies but in terms of safety, the same forces that cause other automobile manufacturers to push their workers to the limit are at work at SIA. Providing a truly safe workplace is beyond their control in a competitive environment where the priority is quotas first rather than safety first.

Capitalist principles still operate in Japanese companies. Flexibility for the company does not begin to translate into flexibility for the workers. When we were hired at SIA, team members were asked to make a commitment to the company. However, ours was an ill-informed commitment. Team members could not have imagined the kind of effort they would expend while "working with others in a fast-paced environment," as the Subaru–Isuzu *Facts and Information* booklet put it. Nor could they envision the negative health effects that routine, expected work tasks would inflict on their bodies.

5

Thinking Like an Associate: Bases of Control

During my first week in the plant, I attended my first department-wide meeting. Its purpose was to present all of us with copies of the company handbook. The handbook explains what the team concept is all about—a workplace based on mutual respect. The focus of the meeting was SIA's managerial philosophy. In order to stress its importance, two representatives from the Operating Committee presented the material. My field notes on that day capture the tone and content of the meeting:

> The meeting was held from 1:00 to 2:15 and run by the Vice President of Human Relations. The Vice President of Manufacturing sat down in front with him. First they had a video of Yamamoto (company president) reading the opening letter in the handbook. Then the VP of Human Relations went through the book with us page by page (a 124-page book!). He stressed that the most important part of the handbook is the corporate character section because that was how they planned to manage the business. (August 3, 1989)

As an acknowledgment of the Japanese management's reputation for providing job security for its workers, we were told how security would be achieved. The Human Relations vice president said, "Job security means many things to different people, but at SIA it means gaining market share and making a profit. This will lead to stable employment."

From the topic of job security we were led into a description of the company's philosophy, the real reason for the meeting. "On page fifteen of the handbook," the vice president said, "there is a good paragraph describing company philosophy." He felt it was so important that he read it aloud to the department: "(8) The Spirit of SIA is Enthusiastic Involvement. Participation and involvement are traditional in American society. Many of us demonstrate this spirit in volunteer activities ranging from Little League baseball and civic groups to church picnics. Why not show this same spirit in our business activities?" Notice how this Japanese company's philosophy relies on American traditions. SIA continually attempted to appear as American as possible by appealing to national symbols of community. That section of the handbook then calls upon Associates to help the company improve society: "SIA has been founded for many purposes—improving the lives of our customers, Associates, and owners, as well as improving society at large. By encouraging every Associate to participate and get involved in the business, SIA will become more useful to society. In the long run, this will also help each of us to grow personally." Through this appeal, the company attempts to connect the worker to something greater than simply holding down a job. SIA's success becomes a mission, an example to set for the rest of society.

Then comes the heart of the message. SIA wants its Associates to involve themselves in the job as they would in the volunteer activities referred to above. What follows is a plea for workers to give all their effort and to focus their entire attention to the success of the company:

> Involve yourself enthusiastically. We are not asking
> Associates to work without compensation, but we do ask that
> all of us help establish a workplace where creativity comes
> naturally. It is natural to cooperate with each other as a team,
> trying to eliminate all possible waste, looking for ways to
> improve, and keeping each one's own work area a clean,
> happy place. After all, work is the place where many of us
> spend an entire third of our 24-hour day, and fully half of our
> waking hours.
>   When people work only to get paid, their workplace
> becomes very uninteresting. When they participate in an
> organization with enthusiasm, however, the very same
> workplace will prove an interesting, even exciting, place for
> them to be. (*SIA Associate Handbook* 1989: 15)

My reaction during the meeting was that the presentation made working for the company sound almost like a spiritual experience—being enthusiastically involved and making a commitment to SIA, the kind of commitment one might make to a church or other voluntary organization. The vice president ended by saying that "the corporate culture at SIA is built on mutual trust."

Even though most of us were skeptical, this sounded like a very different approach to worker-management relations than any of us had experienced. Workers were hopeful that it really would be different. Everyone was optimistic. A new job, good pay, potential for promotion—we were getting in on the ground floor. And the company believed in mutual trust and respect; it seemed too good to be true. It mirrored my first day on the floor, when everyone was so friendly and upbeat:

> My first day in the shop. . . . Both Terry (a teammate from my
> training class) and I had headaches all day. We weren't certain
> if it was from the noise or nerves—although I was not
> nervous. I remember my first day at Farmstead, I almost
> threw up I was so scared. But I wasn't nervous today for
> several reasons. During training we were out in the plant for
> probably three tours and drawing sessions. This helped us get
> acclimated. But more important, people are just plain
> friendly. Being pleasant and considerate to others is really
> stressed in training (remember the KPs in Interaction). . . .
> Another factor is that you come in with your training group
> and you've gotten to know each other during those first three
> weeks. We formed a bond . . . I got to know people's financial
> situation, home situation and many of their aspirations.
> Everyone is really pushing for this job to work for them.
> There is a real sense of optimism. It will be interesting to see
> if this continues. (July 31, 1989)

> Second day in the shop. My team leader is really nice.
> Everyone here is really nice. It is amazing. I believe that after
> the GAT scores, personality was the most critical factor for
> getting hired. (August 1, 1989)

The importance and appeal of workplace participation to enhancing job satisfaction has been documented by research on this subject (Milkman 1991b). Parker and Slaughter (1988) found that at NUMMI workers did not want to go back to the traditional management model. Perhaps some of this enthusiasm for the alternative approach is correlated with the positive atmosphere that is part of the expected behavior and corporate culture under the Japanese model. Management has set a friendlier tone for interaction. When new workers entered the plant, I would ask them how they felt about SIA and if it seemed different from other places where they had worked.

> John said that the only thing that seemed different here were people's attitudes. "But," he said, "we haven't started production yet. Once we do, that will change." John told me that when he was young he could never understand why blue collar workers always had such a negative attitude and were so down on themselves and everybody else. But he said that since he's been working in the real world, he understands. He doesn't agree with them, but he understands how they could get that way because of the job. "You are always told what to do and that you aren't worth anything, until you finally start to believe it." (October 2, 1989)

Based on John's description of working class life, one can begin to understand how the company could turn worker enthusiasm into increased profits. The goal is to create a system of worker compliance. Success depends on management's ability to fashion an environment which appears free of coercion, giving no impetus for resistance. Instead of management devoting time and energy to controlling the workforce directly, workers control themselves. SIA's goal is to gain workers' total cooperation in the company's competitive struggle.

According to Burawoy (1985), companies in advanced capitalist nations organize their system of control in one of two ways, as hegemonic or despotic factory regimes. A company with a despotic system uses coercion as a direct, personal form of control to manage the workforce. He argues that this is inefficient for two reasons. It ignores structural forces which hide the wage relation and work to the benefit of the company; and coercion increases antagonism, resulting in worker resistance and possible unionization. A hegemonic approach is wide-ranging, subtle, and more powerful as it combines coercion with consent. SIA is clearly a company striving for post-Fordist hegemonic control over its workers.

Pre-employment selection, orientation and training for new workers, the team concept, a philosophy of kaizen, shaping shop floor culture from the top down, a computerized assembly line, and just-in-time production comprise the seven components of a multidimensional framework which serves as the basis for SIA's system of compliance. Together, all seven dimensions create a framework that forms a kind of invisible "iron cage" of control over individual workers. Pre-employment selection and orientation and training have already been addressed. This chapter considers the last five dimensions of control, which directly confront workers as they enter the shop floor and which create pressures for conformity to corporate work practices. These conditions make practices such as speedup and working off the clock (when not being paid by the company) more common unless workers collectively resist them. However, resistance is more difficult to develop under the terms established by these hidden dimensions of control.

The Team Concept

The team is the driving structure behind the hegemonic system at SIA. Three levels of worker compliance emerge through the team. At the level of the individual, self-discipline emerges when a worker internalizes the responsibilities of team membership. At the next level of interaction, and if self-discipline fails to spur the worker on, either peer pressure begins to operate or a system of mutual support emerges, depending on the specific circumstances. Finally, if a team member's self-discipline fails and the social pressure exerted by teammates is insufficient, then the team leader or group leader is available to step in and take direct control of the situation.

Compliance through Self-discipline

Self-discipline was a powerful and effective method of control at SIA. In a limited way, identification with one's team would probably occur simply because work is organized around the team and it is a substructure within the plant's authority structure (i.e., company, department, group, team). However, in order to gain hegemony over the workforce, workers must internalize the responsibilities of team membership, which include a sincere desire to help other team members and a commitment to holding up one's own end of the bargain, one's work load. As one of the training instructors put it, "There must be a desire to pull the team up together." Considered in the overall strategy of profit making, if each individual team excels, then the sum of these effects is for the company as a whole to excel.

Team members often pushed themselves to the limit in order to keep up their end of the bargain. Even I internalized the responsibilities of team membership. An example of this occurred during a period when management began altering my station. Each change increased the time it took to complete my series of tasks, forcing me to change other areas of the station in order to keep up. At one point, it simply became impossible to do the amount of work required and I kept falling behind. Even though I knew management had set unrealistic goals for my station, I felt guilty. I found myself literally running around the car in an effort to complete my station and not burden anyone else with my duties.

Compliance through Peer Pressure

Parker and Slaughter were the first to describe the potential power of peer pressure in their analysis of the team concept at NUMMI (1988:22). At SIA, peer pressure emerged as a form of discipline most typically under conditions when a team member chronically failed to keep up with the line. Even though "teaming up" and "pulling together" were part of SIA's official management philosophy, unkind acts toward team members were not necessarily discouraged by management and, at times, they were even encouraged. Team members found that imposing a team structure on a workforce did not automatically lead to cooperation. Emotions countrary to team spirit often surfaced. The following example illustrates a type of peer pressure that was exerted by teammates—behaviors that were encouraged by the company through its team leader training.

A member of our team called Joe regularly made mistakes and fell behind. We were understaffed during this period and each of us was doing at least two and sometimes three stations. Joe was covering two. Because he was having problems, the rest of us observed him and found that he was not following any prescribed order in his tasks. One could not predict which part he might pick up first. In turn, this meant that we never knew which part or parts he might forget. Because our responsibilities included checking the work already completed and correcting any mistakes, Joe's unpredictability increased the level of stress for the team members following him. The team leader and team members worked with him and tried to get Joe to use a system, but he refused.

At one point, team members attempted to convince the team leader to move Joe to another station. Forcing him to master the two situations he had was not worth it to the rest of the team as they were having to catch his mistakes and correct them on top of their own work. The team leader suspected that Joe was simply pretending to be slow and confused in order to get out of working those particular stations. Finally, the team leader devised a scheme to correct the situation and informed the rest of the team of the plan. None of the team members told Joe of the potentially humiliating plan. The team leader informed the rest of us that her plan had been discussed at the monthly Frontline class (a program of ongoing training for team leaders). She said the other team leaders "loved it" and that the Frontline instructor told her to "let him have it." She told us: "I'm going to give him what he wants and watch him screw it up."

According to the plan, on the following day team members were to be shifted to new stations and Joe would be moved to one on the other side of the line, a station that he claimed to prefer. The rest of us were told which stations we would be taking on so that we could review the process sheets for those stations and be prepared for the change. Joe was to be kept in the dark. As it turned out, the plan had to be scrapped as there was an error in line speed and no one was moved. The standoff ended a few days later when a new worker joined our team. The team leader gave up and simply assigned one of Joe's stations to the new worker. When Joe was left with only one station, he was able to do the work. Once he had his station under control, the resentment subsided. The point of the story is that team members cooperated with the team leader in an attempt to force compliance from another team member concerning his job performance.

Cooperating to "bring that member up," which team members had heard emphasized during Orientation and Training, was not Team 1's reaction to Joe. Instead, members cooperated in a scheme to humiliate him. The company, through its ongoing training for team leaders, directly supported an action that was contrary to stated company philosophy: "Everyone at SIA is a team member, and a colleague. We like to use the word 'Associate' to describe this concept, and we intend that every SIA Associate be treated with mutual respect" (*SIA Associate Handbook,* 1989:7).

In addition to the threat of having one's job intensified by the inabilities of another team member, peer pressure emerged from another source—team pride. This was evidenced in the social pressures to keep up a good team image. When one team member appeared inept, it was embarrassing to the whole team because we were held accountable as a team. Since Team 1 was the first team to get the car, we often had an audience observing our work. Even though we were observed by all levels of management from the group leader, car manager, and department manager to members of the Operating Committee, team members were most embarrassed when a Japanese trainer or workers from other teams watched us. We were embarrassed because we knew that the trainers and workers would know for certain when a team member was messing up. It was important to each team member to gain and keep the respect of our Japanese trainer, not only because he was our boss but because we liked him as an individual and had great respect for his knowledge of work and assembling the car. Team members had been informed by one of the interpreters that the trainers were under intense pressure from the head trainer. The interpreter told us that when any team under a trainer's charge made errors, that trainer lost face. Team 1's trainer inspected each car as it left our area. Sometimes he would find as many as thirty defects and when the majority could be attributed to Joe, team members were furious.

Other teams experienced similar feelings of resentment against slower workers. A worker from Team 2 told me that someone he was training on a station was very slow. In reference to that worker's speed he volunteered, "You know, it kind of makes me mad." He said this in a tone indicating he was amazed that he felt that way; it seemed to make him uncomfortable.

Compliance through Mutual Support

Although peer pressure was a large part of SIA's system of control, at the same time I witnessed the emergence of cooperation and mutual support among team members. Support usually surfaced when it was clear that the teammate involved was a victim of the system or that inability to keep up resulted from some outside force. For example, when my station was altered by management and it became impossible to do the amount of work required, two other team members understood my predicament and began to help. They willingly speeded up their stations and worked ahead so that they could help me.

Compliance through Direct Authority

When self-discipline, peer pressure, or mutual support were insufficient to keep the team running at the desired level of production, direct authority from the team leader kicked in. When the chips were down, cooperation was expendable and members were pressured into conforming. After having worked for one month in the plant, I recorded in my notes my impression of the team concept and being a team member. "My gut reaction is that the team leaders are like little corporals stationed throughout the plant. A very effective means of control, when you consider that management's fingers extend down to every seven people (the average team size)."

On the surface, the authority structure at SIA appeared to be an egalitarian and evenhanded system. We were taught in Orientation and Training that groups of concerned individuals would hammer out solutions to problems. If team leaders had problems with discipline, quality, or safety, for example, these could be discussed at the daily team leader meeting (Team 1's group leader held daily meetings with his four team leaders) or at Frontline. One might assume that such a structure would provide for a rational, predictable approach to discipline. One might even expect that a general plant-wide style of discipline would emerge; however, I found this not to be the case.

In reality, each team was unique and subject to its particular team leader's approach to discipline or governance. One of the team leaders in Trim and Final, for instance, was notorious for being extremely dictatorial. Both the workers under him and the material handlers supplying his team expressed contempt for him. (He was eventually promoted to group leader.) At the other end of the spectrum was a Trim and Final team governed by vote. Those team members voted on nearly everything that directly affected them and, according to their team leader, the majority ruled. For example, when a new Associate felt ready to move on to a new station, the whole team would vote on it. The team leader assured me that he determined the topics subject to voting. However, the fact that voting even occurred denotes at least a limited form of democracy. According to that team leader, he knew of no other team in the plant with such a democratic structure.

This diversity in discipline among teams had a contradictory effect on the workforce. On the one hand, it was potentially divisive as many workers resented the fact that some teams received better treatment than others. Often such resentment was expressed in a cynical attitude toward the company; a team member from the "dictator's" team, for instance, described the team concept as a "bunch of bull."

On the other hand, the fact that management allowed diversity to emerge among its team leaders had another, more subtle effect on the workforce. The idea that team leaders were allowed to use their own methods gave an impression that the company was evenhanded because it stood behind its team leaders' personal attempts at getting the job done. Viewed this way, diversity can be seen as part of the company's overall construction of hegemonic control. The only requirement was that whatever the discipline style—voting, cracking the whip, or a laissez-faire attitude—it had to work. As long as their teams succeeded in meeting production quotas, team leaders were left alone.

The style of discipline experienced by Team 1 was mixed. Team members never felt that they were under someone's iron will, yet team suggestions were seldom implemented. One reason suggestions were ignored seemed to be that team leaders were simply afraid of losing control and they saw some suggestions as challenges to their authority. Team leaders themselves were constantly worried about their authority because they were in such an in-between position, intermediaries between the team and management. To illustrate, the following notes describe a meeting that all the team leaders had with management as part of their union awareness program. The notes reveal the considerable frustration team leaders felt about their position:

> This morning as I was getting out my tools, one of the team
> leaders told me about the Friday night meeting. It was a
> required meeting, but the team leaders were not paid. The
> company hosted a hospitality hour and buffet dinner. He said
> it was the nicest buffet he'd ever been to and the booze flowed
> freely. At first people were resentful of being required to
> come, but by the end of the evening everyone was glad that
> they had. The last 15 to 30 minutes the vice president of
> Human Resources asked them to list five things that bothered
> them the most. He said for most people, it was money, but
> for him, it was work overload and lack of authority. Their list
> of five, from most important to least was: (1) They felt the
> responsibilities involved in being team leader deserved more
> pay. (2) Too much work overload; in particular, the amount
> of paper work. (3) The third complaint was the lack of
> authority that the position held. (4) They were expected to be
> everywhere at the same time. They cannot run a process if
> someone is gone and make repairs at the same time. (5) They
> wanted someone to make it clear to the Japanese that our
> work ethic is different from theirs. He said, "We go home to
> see our families in the evenings and we want to spend our
> time with our families on the weekends, not at work." He
> also said that they want all the information that the trainers

have, that they shouldn't be holding information back from
them. (September 25, 1989)

The long work hours and unreasonable demands of which the team
leaders complained have also been documented in auto assembly plants
located in Japan. For example, Kamata's (1973) hidden participant observation at Toyota in Japan reveals a rapid and demanding work pace
and consistently long hours. Kamata describes the physical exhaustion
that Japanese auto workers experience from work intensification and
long daily and weekly hours.

Team 1 members were frustrated by the variations in discipline and
also by uneven implementation of certain company policies. One such
policy was that people were to rotate to the different stations within their
team. Just as discipline varied, so did the way in which this policy was
implemented. On Team 1, the team leader assigned each of us a station
and we worked that station for weeks or months, changing only when
a new Associate was hired. Team members complained bitterly during
morning meetings because the majority of us were experiencing hand and
wrist injuries from the repetitive nature of the work. Team members felt
that injuries might decrease if they rotated on a regular basis. The team
leader refused their requests. When members discussed her refusal among
themselves, they decided she was afraid that the team might fall behind
and cause the line to stop or that defects might increase. (I asked our
Japanese trainer how often people rotated in Japan. He said that it was
on a yearly basis. Perhaps that was another reason the team leader hesi-
tated; the trainer may have discouraged rotation.) Finally, team members
who worked on the last four stations simply took matters into their own
hands and began rotating stations every few hours. Since no problems
occurred, the team leader ignored their behavior and allowed them to
continue. Ironically, SIA's authority structure created a situation where
workers could override the direct authority of their team leader—as long
as it neither interfered with production nor involved any direct, obvious
violations of company policy.

Philosophy of Kaizen

Kaizening is epitomized in the phrase "always searching for a better
way." This was how one vice president described the philosophy of
kaizen during Orientation and Training. Kaizening was accomplished

formally through group meetings or informally when a worker changed some aspect of a station without permission of the team leader or group leader. Directly, kaizening was enforced through periodically decreasing takt time by line speedup, which forced workers to find ways of shaving additional seconds from their tasks. Indirectly, kaizening had a domino effect on the workforce. For example, Team 1 found that making one person's job more efficient often meant shifting part of that process to another worker or team, thereby intensifying someone else's job: an improvement for one person or team often had the opposite effect on another. Team 1 members considered any change to be a kaizen whether it was deemed an improvement or not.

Much to our dismay, Team 1 periodically experienced the consequences of the kaizening in other teams. For example, station one right originally was not a part of our team. It evolved as a result of three separate kaizens from different parts of the plant. First, a team in Paint dumped the job of attaching the torsion bars on Team 1 (a difficult and dangerous job); then came the underbody plugs from chassis; and finally, the protection strips from another team in Trim. Each team had kaizened such that their problems devolved onto Team 1.

For the most part, team members were involved in very little formal kaizening, especially after official start of production. During start-up, team members had kaizened items such as bulletin boards and racks for holding the parts for each station. Team members made signs, constructed a training rack for displaying parts, and built a few devices to make a station safer or faster (such as the short stool on wheels for working under the fender in station five left). On the whole, however, these were fairly benign projects having little direct effect on actual work processes.

A large part of kaizening involved time study. As noted earlier, during training workers were taught to perform time studies on each other and to check against the established standard for each task. When a time study is conducted in a traditional U.S. auto plant, it is performed by management. Workers are not involved in the potentially divisive experience of timing each other's jobs, and union rules protect workers by governing use and implementation of time studies. At SIA, workers sporadically continued to time each other on the shop floor and the process was often used to speed up a person's work. If any time was left after the completion of a station's responsibilities, other tasks or subassemblies could be added, intensifying the job. For example, when two right got his station under control and was able to work ahead, he was given additional duties. He performed rework (work that should be unnecessary, such as repairing or altering parts), for example, putting extra tape on the wiring harnesses. The goal was for workers to be working every second of every minute.

Officially, making decisions while kaizening involved consensus; however, in reality the company's use of consensus in decision making had a contradictory effect on the workforce. The unequal relationship between worker and management made it impossible to reach a consensus that involved more than token input from workers. Since workers had no formal power (i.e., a union) and therefore no recourse, decisions conformed to management's wishes and the topics raised for discussion were determined by management. In this way, the company not only controlled outcomes, it stifled worker input and creative potential.

Although the Japanese system is most consistent with hegemonic control, not every aspect of Burawoy's theory is applicable. For example, "making out"—the idea that workers play games to create spare time yet still make quotas and, by doing so, develop a consensual relationship within production—was effectively undermined at SIA. Instead of a consensual relationship developing through workers' games, kaizening blocked workers from making out in two ways. First, it threatened a worker with constant disruption by suddenly introducing changes in the work station and directly interfering with the making-out process. Just when a worker had a station under control, with a few seconds to spare, he or she ran the risk of having it kaizened. Second, through the kaizen philosophy of continual improvement, management attempted to gain control over workers' creative knowledge and use this to its own advantage. Not only is kaizening designed to capture a worker's secrets for gaining spare time, but once management appropriates that knowledge, it controls when, where, and how those ideas are implemented. Kaizening, therefore, is an extremely effective procedure. It essentially convolutes the making-out process (which under other management systems benefits the worker) into a factor that puts continuous stress on the worker and forces workers' compliance.

Culture of Cooperation through Egalitarian Symbols

SIA's attempt at cultural control was two-tiered. First, at the level of the shop floor, there was an attempt to shape workers' culture through the team structure. Organizing work around the team circumvented the natural formation of small informal work groups, a traditional mechanism of worker solidarity and support (Roy 1960). By formalizing work groups, management created a structure in which team members worked together to meet company goals. If the company could successfully appropriate workers' solidarity and support, then workers would identify their interests with the company's. Daily quotas and speedup placed increased demands on workers and created resentment toward management. The culture of the team was one mechanism for dissipating resistance to those demands. Quite simply, when helping other team members keep up, workers in effect supported the speedup.

Second, at the organizational level, there was an active company-wide campaign to shape organizational culture by elevating the concept of the team and the responsibilities of team membership to the level of the organization. This was part of the company's principle of "driving out fear," as it was expressed in a company handout, an attempt to break down the barriers between workers and management and create a sense of egalitarianism. Team 1's response is reflected in my notes:

> Today Yamamoto (company president) came into our area and apologized to our team leader for not being able to provide enough cars for people to build. Yesterday, at our morning team meeting, Tony had asked the team leader: "Just why is it that Paint can't supply us with cars?" The team leader replied that she would ask someone. Apparently, Yamamoto found out. Since then, the vice president of manufacturing has been on the floor almost all the time. It seems that management is trying to boost morale. We are all extremely tired of the time going so slow. (Team 1 was very impressed that the company president had come down on the factory floor and talked to us in such a friendly, caring manner). (September 14, 1989)

Attempts by the corporation to create a culture of cooperation occurred through specialized language, ideology, ritual, and symbols. In its use of language, certain words and actions which conveyed a sense of equality were repeatedly used. As already emphasized, workers were referred to as Associates, never as workers. Everyone at SIA, from the company president on down, was an Associate. The term was clearly defined throughout the company's literature, notably its booklet *Facts and Information.* At the same time, it was made clear to us that *worker*—and its class aspect representing an adversarial image—was an inappropriate term: "SIA is not hiring workers. It is hiring Associates . . . who work as a team to accomplish a task" (*Facts and Information* 1989:2).

The team metaphor was used at all levels of the company. Each Associate, whether in production or management, was a member of a team, the highest ranking team being the Operating Committee. The team metaphor was clearly portrayed in company documents: "Team leaders are highly skilled Associates, like basketball team captains. They can do all the jobs performed by the members of their team. A group leader is like a coach, responsible for several teams" (SIA and *Facts and Information* 1989:2). The team/sport metaphor was extended to embrace the company's struggle in a competitive market. SIA's corporate character was defined in the *Associate Handbook* through a list of ten company principles, the second being "Together, We Must Beat the Competition." In reference to the team, the company used language to create a sense of caring, part of the responsibility of a good team member. In this way, the company appeared sensitive to the needs of its workers: "SIA believes all Associates should be given a chance to develop to their full physical and mental potential. For this reason, all Associate members will be trained in—and will perform—a number of functions. This increases their value to the team and to SIA" (*Facts and Information* 1989:2).

In addition to the concept of Associate and the ideals associated with being part of the team, both company documents and Orientation and Training instruction focused on caring concepts such as safety, quality, trust, pride, and cleanliness. Team members were encouraged to make such terms a focus of attention. For example, during start-up, teams were directed to make signs for their areas. All of the above concepts were repeated in those signs. Just before SIA's grand opening celebration, Trim and Final Associates were ordered to remove all handmade signs and the majority were taken down; however, at least fifty-five of the signs were not removed. In order for that to have happened, the teams must have made a conscious decision against company policy not to remove those particular signs. (The company wanted them replaced with professional, standardized signs.) The following are some of the slogans that appeared on signs left up after the grand opening, revealing the caring terms which workers found important.

Quality People, Quality Product

Quality and Safety Go Hand in Hand

Safety is Everyone's Concern

Goals of Excellence:
#1 Safe Environment
0 Defects
0 Lost Time Accidents

If You Drop It, YOU Pick It Up

A Little Progress Every Day Adds Up to Big Progress

Steel Toes Required (this included a picture of a shoe)

Moving Conveyer (with a picture of gear teeth chasing a person)

Quality Our #1 Product

Please Remove Rings, Watches and Objects from Pockets

A Sign of Excellence—Team Crafted in Indiana

The SIA Way, Safety in Action

Safety is No Accident (with picture of person in bandages)

Bump Caps Required

Joe Isuzu Says: "You don't need a bump cap, trust me"

Five S's
1. Seriri—A place for everything
2. Seiton—Everything in its place
3. Seiketsee—Tools, orderly and clean
4. Shitukarie—Team discipline
5. Shitsuke—Intense training

Code of Conduct:
Start Meeting on Time
Stay on Subject
One Speaker at a Time
Speak Loud Enough so Others Hear
Don't Leave Meeting to Talk with Others
NO Idea is a Bad Idea
Pay Attention to Speaker
Use Common Sense

Don't Take Short Cuts (hung in the pit area)

Herbie says: "Don't be late, the line won't wait"

Clean Up for a Better Tomorrow
1. If you see it, pick it up
2. Safety and good work habits go hand in hand
3. Let's all pitch in and take the time to keep your area clean

Quality is SIA's Way of Life. Let's all work together to keep SIA clean.

Break Area (sketch of coffee mug)

Quality Pays in Many Ways (drawing of cash register)

Keep Doors Closed When Not in Use (on door of broom closet)

If You Do It Right, You Won't Need the Light (drawing of red and yellow lights which light up when the cords are pulled)

On Team 1, one other woman team member and I were usually directed to work on signs while the men team members were directed to build racks. Often, the team leader or group leader would suggest a specific item for a sign, but we were usually left on our own as to how to convey the message. Their requests often involved safety or quality. The team leader said that the Japanese were "very big on signs" and that at Subaru in Japan signs hung everywhere.

Symbols related to forms, shapes, and experiences were consciously manipulated to convey a sense of egalitarianism. Everyone, from the company president on down, wore the same basic uniform, parked in the same general parking lots, ate in the same cafeteria, and was restricted to a half-hour lunch period. All Associates experienced the same orientation. Clerical and management Associates worked together in one large room without barriers—similar to the other departments within the plant.

SIA used rituals and ceremonies to create a shared experience of belonging. These included morning exercises and daily team meetings. The huddle ritual, with its inspirational message and hand clasp, conveyed a sense of belonging, physically bringing us together as a team. Through the huddle we signified our unity before the beginning of each day's work. There were also dramatic public and private ceremonies to celebrate different steps in the growth of the company. For example, there was a ceremony to commemorate the first car and truck to come off the line. The presidents of Fuji Heavy and Isuzu arrived from Japan for formal inspection of the first vehicles. They made speeches and sponsored a picnic for everyone in the plant to celebrate what they referred to as an historic occasion. In addition to formal ceremonies, the Japanese trainers sponsored parties to celebrate the official start of production.

After SOP, SIA had a grand opening celebration which was laden with images of nationalism and team spirit. The celebration was held in a large white tent just outside the plant. The Purdue University marching band played and baton twirlers performed while specially invited guests from the surrounding communities took their seats. Finally, as part of the opening ceremony, a curtain parted at the back of the stage and SIA Associates marched across the stage four abreast through a haze of smoke while the company song "Team Up for Tomorrow" played over the speaker system. The audience, which included the governor and local dignitaries, applauded and gave the Associates a standing ovation. An Associate from Team 2 told me, "It seems kind of like graduation." I might have compared it more to a military parade. In addition to the grand opening, the company held an Associates' Day just for plant employees and their families. Families were fed, entertained with clowns and singers, and given tours of the plant.

Despite these efforts to promote the expected company loyalty and cooperation, workers did not always go as far as the company desired:

> Today was spent cleaning for the week of the grand opening
> ceremony and tours. A rehearsal was scheduled after work
> from 3:15 to 5:00 for all Associates. We are to practice
> forming a "river of Associates" for the dedication ceremonies
> on Monday. Terry was the only person I know of that
> attended the rehearsal. Everyone else was put out because it
> was scheduled after work. (October 13, 1989)

> Even though attendance was "strongly recommended," Terry
> said that way less than half of the plant was there. The
> trainers outnumbered the workers. (October 15, 1989)

The last plant-wide activity in which I was involved was the SIA New Year's party (there was no Christmas party). The company president and vice president of manufacturing spoke and then they danced with a few Associates in a relaxed atmosphere. All of these rituals, symbolic acts, dramatic ceremonies, and private celebrations allowed Associates to experience a common connection with SIA and acknowledged important events in the company's history.

Another symbolic ritual was the department meeting. During my six-month tenure at SIA there were seven department-wide meetings, including both the car and truck sides, and there was one additional meeting in which only the car side participated. The meetings were not held regularly; they were usually in response to some issue such as start-up or the problems in the Paint department. They were commonly held the last hour of the day. During these meetings Trim and Final Associates were briefed on the status of production, quality, safety, or some related topic. The assembly line would be shut down and all of the workers in the department would make their way across the room to the cafeteria. Teams usually sat together, smoked, and drank sodas in a relaxed environment while the manager attempted to create a feeling of team spirit, firing up the players like a coach at a pep rally before a big game. In the meeting held just before SOP, the Trim and Final manager solemnly stated: "We are finally entering into the competition . . . the company has done everything to prepare us for this moment . . . now it is up to us to beat it [the competition]."

The Computerized Assembly Line

The aforegoing five components (selection, orientation and training, team concept, philosophy of kaizen, and egalitarianism) emphasize the social control features of the Japanese model. The final components in SIA's multidimensional scheme—the assembly line and just-in-time production—are factors associated with technical control of work.

The assembly line has long been recognized as a means of direct, technical control over workers due to its ability to set the pace of work. In the Japanese model, the computerized assembly line differs from a traditional assembly line in that it provides additional means of scrutiny and discipline over the workforce.

At SIA, the computerized assembly line with its technical control over the pace of work directly determined the quality of a worker's day. A good day contained several unpredicted line stoppages (down time). Usually when the line stopped unexpectedly, team members would find a way to visit and relax. The line set the physical pace of our work; however, it was not simply the line and its direct control that drove us. The social pressure of team membership also helped to chain us psychologically to the line.

> Working on the line is so intense. You are under constant
> pressure. . . . Henry and I try to talk and joke a little bit as we
> work across from each other, to try and break up the
> intensity. . . . We all take our jobs seriously and do our best,
> but there is a line dividing us in the way some of us feel about
> the work and how others see it. The team leader is totally
> wrapped up in SIA as a company. Henry, Terry, and Karen
> see it more as a job. (September 21, 1989)

As described in chapter four, the mainframe computer system driving the assembly line could focus everyone's attention on any team that fell behind. A worker having difficulty pulled a yellow cord located above the line at each station. The instant the cord was pulled, that team's music was played over the loudspeaker system and continued until the cord was pulled again by the team leader signaling that things were under control. If the line stopped, the music continued until it began moving once again. The music identified the team and focused department-wide attention on whichever team had a problem. In addition to the social pressure created through identifying a team by its music, the computer system kept track of the number of times each team pulled the cord and how long the line was stopped. Such a system of "bookkeeping" allowed management to put tremendous pressure on specific teams. Heavy emphasis was placed on achieving perfect daily records with no down time or defects. If any team had a chronic problem, it became a topic of discussion by other teams and group leaders. On various mornings when our group leader participated in Team 1's morning meeting, he often discussed problems that other teams were experiencing and at one meeting shortly after SOP (September) he informed us that we were the only team still experiencing down time. Team 1 had been singled out as the team with the problem—and as the team to be pressured into conformity. Ironically, before SOP Team 1 was praised for its quality. We were keen on discovering and correcting every defect before allowing the car body to leave our area.

> Our team leader said that she heard a rumor that we had the
> best team in the plant. I asked her where she heard it because
> I was wondering what constituted the "best." She said that it

came from IPC inspection people. Apparently, we have the least rework of any team. She said it really made her proud that Team 1 had such a reputation. (August 22, 1989)

Team 1 was experiencing the contradiction between the company's expectation of high quality and its demand for increased production.

Just-in-Time Production

In addition to the computerized assembly line, team members experienced technical control through the application of just-in-time system of inventory control. It had the effect of directly intensifying and speeding up team members' work. As mentioned in chapter four, just-in-time production put the burden of parts shortages on line workers and material handlers. With just-in-time, parts for assembling the cars and trucks are not brought onto the premises until the last possible moment, shifting the burden of stockpiling and quality control to parts suppliers. Line workers were put in the position of scrambling for parts, never certain when they would be delivered or if they would make it to the line in time. In theory, all parts on the line had been quality inspected by the vendor and were ready for use. In reality, team members were forced to alter many of the parts. For example, team members had to cut an additional opening in the toeboard insulator and they also put additional tape wrapping on wiring harnesses. Just-in-time production often forced speedup when workers were forced to work down the line to install parts that arrived late or when they were forced to modify a part before it could be installed.

Each of the five dimensions of management control described here helped create compliance to company norms and goals. On the other hand, each control dimension also created conditions that inherently contradicted SIA's philosophy of egalitarianism. For example, the direct control of the team leader provoked resentment among team members who had expectations of a rationalized, evenhanded approach to discipline. The intentional use of peer pressure had the potential to undermine team solidarity. Kaizening did not necessarily result in greater efficiency, and as Team 1 discovered, it could have the opposite effect. Finally, the Fordist thrust of technically advanced work processes, such as the computer-controlled assembly line and just-in-time production, were direct barriers to instituting a company philosophy of fairness, cooperation, and egalitarianism. Even so, these work processes were the major forces shaping the daily reality of a worker's world in a Japanese automobile transplant. The multidimensional structure of control at SIA created a framework that enforced compliance from the individual worker; however, as workers experienced contradictions within this system of control, worker resistance began to emerge.

6

Working Like a Worker: Bases of Resistance

The team leaders are very enthusiastic about the team concept. The team leaders from Teams 1, 2, and 3 each take their jobs very seriously. . . . I was repairing a ceiling wire harness in Team 2's area today. Ike from Team 2 pointed out to me that a clip was missing so I found one and taped it to the harness. While I was working on the harness, the team leader from Team 2 came up to me and gave me a short lecture on how this is the way we work best as a team—"picking up someone else's mistake and letting them know it before it hits the end of the line and you are held accountable." I got basically the same lecture from the team leader on Team 3. He contacted me because I've been covering up a hole in the ceiling where the sun visor screws into the body. He showed me where it was and said, "This is how teams work together." All the team leaders are so patronizing and paternalistic. I think it must be the way they are taught to handle us in their Frontline sessions (monthly training for team leaders). (September 20, 1989)

Two months later:

The team leader from Team 2 told John and me that he is really depressed with how things are going. He said, "I thought this place would be different with its team concept and all, but management is just trying to work people to death." (November 20, 1989)

During the six months that I worked in the plant I witnessed a visible change in worker behavior. Over a period of time, team members withdrew their active participation from company rituals and resorted to open acts of defiance and resistance against management and company philosophy. Of course, some workers undoubtedly were resistant toward management before they came to SIA; however, no one outwardly displayed this when I first began working in the plant. Instead, workers seemed to have high hopes that the training instructors' message was true—that SIA was different from other companies because its management style was based on an egalitarian, team philosophy with worker participation being an integral part of that. The general change in behavior occurred shortly after the official start of production (SOP) in September, when our overall work experience became tied to the assembly line.

The work we performed before SOP involved getting the kinks out of the production process. During this initial start-up period and even for a few weeks after SOP, there were problems in the Paint department which drastically cut back on the number of cars we received to work on. During this time, Team 1 kept busy training, making signs, building racks, designing the physical layout of our stations, meeting other workers, and observing other teams while they trained. Even though the atmosphere was easygoing, team members grew bored with killing time and eagerly anticipated getting enough cars from Paint for us to work on the line. However, once the team got its wish and experienced the reality of being chained to the line for eight hours a day, attitudes quickly changed and team members expressed their desire for just a few of those slow days before SOP. As one aptly put it: "I just pray for someone to pull the red cord." This reaction to assembly line work is the same response workers described fifty years ago. Chinoy's 1955 study of auto workers documents that they would cheer when the line went down, as long as it was not for long enough to get them sent home.

As line speed increased, pressure mounted and behavior toward management and the company began to change. Before SOP, team members generally participated in company rituals and upheld the philosophy of cleanliness, kaizening, and quality. After SOP, life was a different story.

Evidence of resistance emerged in various individual and collective forms. Individual resistance was expressed through silent protest when workers refused to participate in company rituals and in the form of complaints through anonymous letters written to the company as part of SIA's program of rumor control. Collective resistance emerged as sabotage when workers surreptitiously stopped the assembly line. Team members protested unfair company policies by refusing to participate in team meetings. At the team and group levels, resistance took the form of direct confrontation when workers refused management requests. At the department and plant-wide levels, resistance assumed the form of organized agitation.

The transformation in the behavior of workers hired after SOP was very rapid, often surfacing within a few weeks. By contrast, those of us hired before SOP worked for several months before active resistance emerged. When a new team member entered the plant, he or she was generally quite enthusiastic about the team philosophy and its prescribed rituals. Typically, new members actively participated in morning team meetings by making suggestions that might improve the station where they were training. This activity was part of kaizening. Sometimes it seemed as though new members actually searched for topics to bring up for discussion. Of course, one reason that they had so many suggestions was simply because of their newness. For example, Terry and I started working on Team 1 at the same time. During our first few weeks, we found ourselves discussing how some stations needed improvements which seemed obvious to us and we wondered why the rest of the team had not noticed. Our fresh perspective allowed us to see things which experienced workers overlooked. Even though new members showed the most enthusiasm, until SOP the rest of Team 1 also continued to participate in discussions at the morning team meetings.

The morning team meeting was a ritual of cooperation used as a mechanism to connect management to worker. Through these meetings Team 1 received status reports in the form of the daily defect sheet from management. This report involved the team in the flow of information and gave the appearance that all of us were privy to information customarily confined to management. We were part of one big, company team. Each team member carefully examined the defect sheet to see how Team 1 compared to the other teams in Trim and Final. After SOP, when the team leader passed around the defect report sheet, instead of carefully examining and reacting to it, team members quietly handed it from one person to another without glancing at it.

Another ritual from which team members withdrew their participation occurred just before the closing of every meeting when the team leader would ask if anyone had anything to say. The team leader would turn to each member and nod as a gesture of encouragement. Initially, team members would bring up topics for discussion. After SOP, as the team leader turned to each of us, everyone remained silent.

After SOP, team members complained that the morning meeting had little practical application. When we were finally under a steady production schedule, the meeting was limited to five minutes and its ritualistic function became apparent. It served no practical purpose for the team. The start of production revealed the inherent contradiction of a meeting that took time away from production. It was ultimately squeezed into the fewest minutes possible so that its practical value as a potential forum for solving problems became virtually nonexistent.

The growth of frustration and resentment among team members sometimes led to confrontations with team leaders. For example, one morning in November, Team 1 members held a meeting while the team leader was absent and formulated a list of demands to submit to the team leader, focusing on issues of how the team was controlled.

> Our team leader went to Frontline all day today and left Terry in charge. . . . In the afternoon we had a meeting when the line stopped early and the team decided that they wanted to tell the team leader some things as a group. Terry took notes and left them on her desk. There were four items: (1) We want to rotate each week with women doing 1 left and men doing 1 right (they won't let women do the torsion bars on 1 right). (2) We want a team meeting right after the line stops each day to discuss problems. (3) We want to be informed about policies that are in the making (such as the attendance policy that was made without our input). (4) We don't want the morning meeting to start before 6:30 in the morning (currently, it starts right after exercises and before the bell). Everyone agreed on all the items; none of them were suggested by me. (November 6, 1989)

In many instances double standards that emerged in implementation of policies increased workers' resentment of company rules, as illustrated in the following example. In November a team member attempted to circulate a card for a friend from her orientation class. The friend's wife was having a baby and, since she had been pregnant before he was hired at SIA, they had no health insurance to cover the birth. The Team 1 member wanted to take up a collection to help defray some of the cost. While circulating the card, the team member was informed by the team leader that she would be fired if she continued because of the "no solicitation rule." This brought the immediate reply: "What about the company soliciting for United Way?" (Solicitation for this charitable organization occurred on company time and many workers complained that the company was overly aggressive in getting them to contribute.) The team leader agreed with the team member and attempted to get special permission from Human Resources to circulate the card. They replied that it had to be done on the worker's own time. The team leader informed the team that the policy was connected to SIA's union awareness program. Ironically, the next day during a break, the team leader asked each of us to contribute five dollars toward a Christmas party with the Japanese trainers. One team member remarked: "This sounds like solicitation." The team leader replied: "Yes, but it's on my own time." A second team member shot back: "Yeah, but this is our time too and I don't want to hear about it." The team leader sat down.

Silent protest was a common form of resistance and one target of such protest was morning exercises. About five minutes before the start of the shift, music was played over the loudspeaker system and all of us in Trim and Final lined up with our team or group to perform stretching exercises. During my first few months at SIA most team members regularly participated. However, after SOP the company took away a five-minute cleanup period at the end of the shift. In response, Team 1 refused to exercise. Some members would arrive at the plant after exercises were over. Others simply sat at the break table while the music played. The exercises were a relatively safe target of protest because they occurred before the start of the shift. Although the pressure to cooperate and conform to company wishes was constant, workers legally had the right to refuse.

Sending an anonymous letter was a weak form of resistance because it involved little risk to the individual. It utilized a formal procedure instituted by the company. As part of their "fair treatment policy," the company distributed prestamped, self-addressed envelopes for people to write in anonymously with questions or comments. The comments were posted throughout the plant on special bulletin boards with both the worker's comment and the company's reply. Between October 26, when the first batch was posted, and January 5, 150 comments, questions, and complaints were aired. At first they were optimistic, containing questions concerning the future. For example, people asked if there would be a credit union, a car purchase program, day care facility, or a fitness gym.

Later the anonymous letter system became a sounding board for complaints and dissatisfaction. Concerns emerged over scheduling overtime without notification. Parents complained that meetings scheduled after work and long hours of overtime conflicted with their children's hours at day care. Workers also expressed concern that favoritism existed in parking, lunch hours, bonus plans, scheduling of overtime, and the loaning out of company cars. There were repeated complaints that group and team leaders were being chosen without any job postings. Trim and Final Associates wanted to know why Maintenance Associates were paid two dollars more per hour. There were repeated concerns that quality was being sacrificed in order to meet daily quotas. Workers questioned why seniority was used for some things, such as enrollment in the pension plan, but not for transfers and promotions. One worker wanted to know why security checks were unequally applied as workers with lunch boxes were searched when leaving through the front door while those with briefcases were not checked. Another worker quoted state law concerning overtime pay, stressing it was illegal for the company to require workers to clean their areas and put their tools away after the shift had ended. There were also the more predictable complaints concerning the food and long lines in the cafeteria and about uniforms, gloves, and plant temperature. However, the nature of many of the comments revealed that the company was not totally successful in instituting a spirit of cooperation and a culture of egalitarianism.

Some collective resistance was expressed through jokes and humor, team members making light of company rituals and the philosophy of kaizen. As earlier described, during the team huddle ritual at the end of each team meeting, the team leader would call upon a team member to share an inspirational message before the beginning of our day's work. Some members told jokes, making light of what was presented to us as a fairly solemn ritual. Another example of making light of rituals occurred at morning exercises when workers would jump around and act silly. Kaizening, the company's philosophy of continuous improvement, was also the brunt of team jokes. When the line stopped, a team member would suggest: "Let's kaizen that chair," or if something really went wrong, a member might say, "I guess they kaizened that!"

SIA's unilateral decision to run the assembly line right up to the moment the shift ended resulted in more than one act of collective resistance. During Orientation and Training, team members were told that workers would participate in policy formation, and that "communication was a two-way street." In reality, team members found that policies were routinely instituted from the top down with no input from anyone below the level of team leader; often even team leaders expressed surprise at new policies. The following incident illuminates this point.

By early December the line was moving steadily and Trim and Final was building about sixty cars a day. During the week of December 4, the company instituted a policy of running the line right up until the buzzer sounded to signify quitting time. Until then, team members had been given about five minutes at the end of the day to finish the stations, clean up their areas, and put away tools. The group leader held a joint meeting with Team 1 and Team 2 at which he warned that this change was going to take place and attempted to gain our cooperation. He asked us to support the policy by picking up our tools and locking them in the tool cabinet after the line stopped. (Tools not locked up disappeared. It was rumored that the Japanese trainers from the truck line borrowed them, and there was no time for tracking them down.)

At the meeting, several workers from both teams reacted strongly to the group leader's request for cooperation. A worker from Team 1 said, "This is the kind of bullshit that brings in a union." A second remarked, "This place is getting too Japanese around here; pretty soon they will be asking us to donate our Saturdays." A Team 1 member said, "This is America, not Japan, and we get paid here." A Team 2 member assured the group leader that he was "not a volunteer." Other members explained that cleanup involved more than simply unhooking a tool and putting it away. One worker had nine tools and also had to cover all of the brake lines by wrapping them in plastic. They attempted to convince the group leader that they used the five minutes after the line stopped to get caught up and organized for the next day: "So our processes don't get screwed up." As a group, they were adamant that they would not work after the buzzer. At this point, the group leader informed us that the decision had been made higher up and it was his responsibility to gain our cooperation. Team members could see that he was under pressure but everyone remained committed in opposition to the new rule.

On the following day, the line continued moving until the buzzer sounded. As it happened, I was so far behind that when the line stopped, I did not realize the buzzer had sounded and I kept working. As two teammates walked by, one called to me, "Laurie, don't do it!" I put down my tools. As I was leaving, I overheard our team leader ask another team member a question concerning work. He replied, "Look, it's after 3:00. I don't know," and he walked on by. From that day on, whenever the line ran up to quitting time, all of us on the team dropped whatever we were doing and immediately walked out, leaving the team leader to lock up the tools and clean the area. At one team meeting the team leader complained that she had stayed until 5:30 P.M. cleaning up and putting away our tools. One team member responded, "She was crazy to do it, and we weren't going to."

Several examples of collective resistance also emerged in response to management's unilateral scheduling and unscheduling of overtime. In December, both the car and truck sides were trying to meet the year-end production quotas. In a one-week period several events occurred that crystallized worker resentment and led to an act of collective resistance. On Tuesday we were told that we would work all day on Saturday. The following morning the car manager informed us that we would work nine hours that day and for the next two days so we would not have to work Saturday. At the same time, however, he assured us that if there were too many unscheduled line stoppages, we would also end up working Saturday after all. In response, one team member said, "They're just trying to screw us out of eight hours of overtime." On Friday morning, they informed us that we would only work our regular eight-hour shift. However, when the three o'clock buzzer sounded, the line continued to move. Instead of staying with the line, nearly everyone on the car side put on a coat and walked out. As it turned out, the line moved for only another minute or so, but no one in Trim and Final knew this. To leave a moving line was a direct act of resistance and a cause for firing.

On the truck side of Trim and Final, overtime scheduling was an even bigger issue because they had to meet larger monthly production quotas (ours were reduced because of the problems in Paint). In the middle of December, I talked about overtime scheduling with a truck line worker from my training class. On the previous day, her group leader had told her team at 2:50 P.M. that the truck line would work until 4:00 P.M. At 3:00 P.M. they were given no break (even though stated company policy provided for a five-minute break at 3:00 P.M. when working overtime), so they could not even call home. She was particularly upset because her young son came home from school to an empty house. At 4:00 P.M. the line was not stopped. It did not stop until 4:50 P.M. She said that several members of her team started leaving at 4:00 P.M., even though the line was still moving. The group leader literally chased them down and got them back to work by threatening to fire them.

Overtime scheduling and the company's response to workers exercising their rights according to company policy triggered a direct confrontation between management and the women members of Team 1. Two days before December vacation, the car manager decided to work Trim and Final overtime with virtually no advance notice. Our team leader asked us, individually, whether or not we were willing to stay over. I declined and so did another woman on my team. Previously, the company had handed down a policy concerning overtime which stated that "scheduled" and "emergency" overtime were mandatory but "unscheduled" overtime was not. Scheduled was defined as having been announced by the end of the shift on the previous day. Therefore, in this case, the overtime was unscheduled and we had the right to refuse.

That afternoon, the group leader approached me and asked why I was not willing to work. I explained that I had not expected to work and had a medical appointment. Shortly after that, our team leader informed us that, "according to human resources, if we left at 3:00 P.M., it would be an unexcused absence." The company was instituting this policy on the spot. This caused a third woman on our team also to refuse the overtime. It was obvious to her that the company was simply fabricating the policy to force us to work. On principle, she decided to leave with us to protest the company's method of assigning unexcused absences. Now three members were leaving. When the group leader learned this, he informed the car manager that there would not be enough people to keep the line moving.

At this point, the car manager approached me with the group leader by his side and said, "Look, here at SIA we are trying to be different. If this was any other place, I wouldn't bother to talk to you. I'd just tell the group leader to tell you to work or else. I don't want to get into a position where I am talking discipline with an employee, because I know you are a good worker. I've seen you work." I replied that this was not scheduled overtime and he himself had said it was not an emergency, so how could he discipline me? He said, "Anyone who leaves the line while it is moving is in jeopardy of being fired." When he finished with me I told a team member to warn the others to be prepared for some intimidation. The other team member was already in tears. Her reason for crying: "Because it just wasn't fair," and she was still going to leave.

At this juncture, our team leader made a surprising announcement, telling the car manager that she was also leaving in protest. He put immediate pressure on her, in front of the team, informing her that she was putting her job in jeopardy if she left. The women held their ground. Finally, when faced with the intended departure of four team members and the fact that this would shut the line down, management backed down. I suggested to the manager that if he agreed that no one would get an unexcused absence for leaving (at this time we did not even know what the ramifications were of an unexcused absence—no policy had been established), both the team leader and the other protester would agree to stay. They accepted those terms; I and the other woman who needed to leave left. The next day our teammates informed us that only three cars were built after we left. They described the demands made on us as a "power play by management." Our resistance to overtime was seen as a rejection of the company's philosophy of forced cooperation.

Sabotage occurred when workers on one of the car line teams discovered how to stop the assembly line without management tracing their location. Whenever one of their team members fell behind and the "coast was clear" (no team leaders or group leaders in sight), they stopped the line and the entire car side went down. This not only allowed people on their team to catch up, it gave everyone time away from the line. In addition, it provided entertainment as workers watched management scramble around trying to find the source of the line stoppage. At one morning team meeting, our team leader reported that the line had stopped for a total of twenty minutes the day before and the company was unable to account for the time. Clearly, that team was taking a chance; however, the workers who were aware of the sabotage never told management. Whether the reason for complicity was selfish, because of the appreciated breaks, or was based on loyalty to other workers, their silence was a direct act of resistance and evidence of lack of commitment to the company.

A plant-wide form of collective resistance emerged in the form of organized agitation at team and department meetings. Workers decided informally on this plan of action in order to fight the company's intended policy of shift rotation. Management announced the policy and stated that it was "not up for discussion." All workers would have to rotate when the second shift was added. This infuriated many workers. Several people stated that it was typical of the kinds of decisions in which workers had no say. Many things that had a direct effect on workers' lives, such as overtime, line speed, and shift rotation, were not up for discussion. The essence of the participation workers were granted involved, at best, improving quality; at worst and more commonly, it involved speeding up their jobs.

Concerning shift rotation, workers informally passed the word around the plant to "keep the pressure on by bringing it up at meetings." Word was passed by several means. For example, workers from the Paint department regularly entered Team 1's area to pick up parts that were reused by Paint; Team 1 members talked to material handlers on a daily basis; workers from Body circulated around various teams to examine problems with tolerance; team members remained in contact with work-

ers from their training classes; and women team members became part
of an informal network of women who exchanged information (Gottfried and Graham 1993). In this way, a network for passing and sharing
information built up throughout the plant.

When workers determined that the dissatisfaction was plant-wide, the
issue of shift rotation was brought up almost daily at morning team meetings and at department meetings. As described in chapter five, my first
department meeting, during my first week in the plant, was for the purpose of distributing and explaining the employee handbook. The SIA philosophy of "respect for people, commitment to safety, and quality in
everything we do" was emphasized, and the company's ten operating
principles were presented:

1. SIA is made up of its people—*We* are the corporation.
2. Together, we must beat the competition.
3. Job security is important to all of us.
4. Quality is the top priority.
5. We must eliminate *muda* (waste) throughout the
   company.
6. Kaizen means searching for a better way.
7. Each of us should strive to be a multitalented person.
8. The spirit of SIA is enthusiastic involvement.
9. Open communications build mutual trust.
10. We build Hoosier pride into every vehicle.

We were told that the operating principles (examined more fully in chapter three) expressed SIA's philosophy and its long-range view of how we
would attain our mission. As recorded in my field notes, during the meeting a representative from management stated: "We were to pull in the
same direction and share information. Communication at SIA was two-
way with no third parties. Corporate culture was built on mutual trust."

Toward the end of the meeting the department manager asked for
questions. Of a total of nineteen questions asked, nearly half—nine—
concerned shift rotation and the status of hiring for the shifts. Several
people called it "unfair" that we had no input into the shift rotation
decision. One worker complained that rotating between first and second
shifts would interfere with college classes. Someone followed up on the
issue of education by asking if we could get training before moving to
second shift so that we could use our education benefit. Another asked

how we could do volunteer activities if we were rotated to second shift. Another expressed concerns about scheduling day care.

The issue continued to surface at team and department meetings. Workers questioned the company's principle of two-way communication and its claim to be different from other places where they had worked. They expressed indignation at how the company was failing to play by its own rules. The pressure continued. Eventually, management changed its ruling: one morning an announcement was made by the team leader at a team meeting that there would be no shift rotation.

Collective resistance also emerged over health and safety issues. In October, Human Resources held a department-wide meeting with Trim and Final to inform workers about the "right to know" law concerning hazardous materials in the workplace. During the question-and-answer period an Associate who worked in the tire bay complained that it had taken him four months to find out the contents of the hydraulic fluid in his machine. (The fluid was from Japan, so there were no papers on it.) During those four months, he said, the machine had regularly broken down. He described how the fluid had gotten all over him. Finally, he found out that the fluid contained lead and his group leader taught him the proper precautions to use when handling it. The tire bay worker's point was to make sure all of us knew that he had been exposed to the substance for four months.

Following the lead exposure complaint, a worker asked: "Do we have the right to refuse to work with a chemical if there is no information sheet on it?" The person from Human Resources brushed off his question, so I asked: "What if I was afraid to work with a chemical and there was no information sheet on it? Do I have the right to refuse to do the job?" His reply: "You always have the right to quit." Several workers became angry at his response. One woman called out: "She doesn't want to quit; she just is afraid of the chemicals." Another person complained to him: "You are not answering her question." A male worker demanded: "Does SIA have a policy on it?" The reply: "I don't have the answer to your questions." At the end of the meeting the Human Resources representative asked us all to sign a statement attached to our booklets stating that we understood the law. One person said: "I can't sign this because I don't understand the law, and just what is meant by the right to know." People crowded around me after the meeting and said that they had turned in their sheets without signatures.

In general, the weakest forms of worker resistance were individual and often called for no action by the company. The most effective forms tended to be collective, involved some risk to the individuals involved, were goal directed, and challenged the company's claim to fairness and equality. In my experiences at SIA, it appeared that planned collective action was not necessarily more effective for achieving desired results than was spontaneous collective action. Possibly this was because spontaneous action could be interpreted as a direct indication of the importance that workers placed on a particular issue. Spontaneous collective action was not only a show of worker solidarity but also indicated a certain level of militancy, as it reflected workers' willingness to engage in risky behavior without knowing if others would join in the action. In sum, both planned and spontaneous actions expressed a collective will in direct opposition to management's authority. In their resistance to unfair rules and policies, workers turned the company's ideology of egalitarianism, its effort to create a culture of cooperation, and its claim to be different from U.S. plants to their own advantage. Their acts of resistance became righteous acts of indignation as they exposed how the company failed to play by its own rules. The workers' success in preventing mandatory shift rotation, their resistance to working unscheduled overtime, and their refusal to work off the clock exemplify how they used resistance to negotiate and how they cooperated on their own terms.

The limitation of the company's hegemonic approach is revealed in all of these examples. As the company set up rules and regulations to conform with the demands of production in a capitalist environment, it became apparent that SIA was just like any other company operating within the same constraints. When faced with the pressures of production quotas, management resorted to intimidation, threats, and, when necessary, through its Human Relations department, created policies on the spot in order to get what it wanted. It became clear to workers that the company was always willing to repress their concerns to expedite production goals. Only when workers stood their ground, in solidarity, were they able to force management to capitulate—or in some cases simply adhere to formal preexisting company policies.

7

Voices from the Floor

One goal of this project was to explore life on the shop floor as seen by workers. As a point of departure for this chapter, I returned to some of the current workers in 1994 and asked them to read the earlier chapters and share their reactions with me.

I distributed the manuscript to six readers, all from the Trim and Final department. Readers included both truck and car line workers as well as first and second shift workers. Two were women; I was unable to contact any minority workers. Two were prounion, two antiunion, and two undecided. All were Associates, none temporary workers. The readers ranged in age from their early 20s to mid-40s. Four completed the entire manuscript. I interviewed the readers both before and after they read the manuscript. So I have six initial interviews and four more upon completion. In addition I interviewed two other workers who were not asked to read the manuscript. The interviews took place between January 19, 1994 and February 20, 1994. All interviews involved open-ended questions and took place either in person or by phone.

One reason for contacting current workers was to find out if the period of data collection was too time specific. I feared that the events documented here might be anomalous, arising from kinks that had to be worked out during the first year of production. It was important to discover if my findings were relevant to people currently working in the plant.

The reactions of those interviewed were both interesting and instructive:

> Reader one: I'd say things are pretty much the same.
>
> Reader two: I don't disagree with anything factual. We have

a disagreement on unions. You came from a prounion standpoint. Factually, no disagreement; it seemed accurate.

Reader three: You are sneaky! I never had a clue! I saw a little hostility, kind of biased. You think the company is taking advantage. I don't think you are wrong. I had the feeling when I was hired that I would do whatever they wanted. You seemed kind of negative. There is a gap between those really running the place and the executives. Workers are only warm bodies.

One of the readers wrote and signed the following statement: "I agree with Laurie's interpretation of the events described in the manuscript. For the most part, I believe that a lot of these issues are still relevant. However, I am in a different area now, and things have improved for me."

As these responses illustrate, continuity rather than change appears to be a dominant aspect of these workers' experiences since I completed my initial research. The purpose of this chapter is to revisit and link together the central themes of the book, as related both to the specific experiences of SIA workers and to the more general issue of corporate control over labor. Excerpts from 1994 interviews with SIA workers are used to provide shop floor perspectives on my findings and to illustrate the commonalities and nuances of workers' experiences under the Japanese model.

Following is a reconsideration of the debate concerning the nature of the Japanese model. The arguments of theorists who assert that it is merely a refinement of Fordism are contrasted with my view that it represents a significant shift to a post-Fordist hegemonic form of corporate control. I then turn to the contrasts between what I see as the underlying purpose of the Japanese model and the purposes served by the model's image of cooperation and worker autonomy. Worker's views of the model are then addressed to explore their reactions to work life under the Japanese model. Key issues of work intensification and safety illustrate how and why the idealized image and ideology of the Japanese model are constantly undermined by workers' shop floor experiences. Finally, I speculate on the prospects for unionization in U.S. transplants.

Does the Japanese Model Represent a New System of Management?

As noted in the first chapter, analysts disagree over the nature of the Japanese model's impact on workers: does the model represent a new system of management or is it is simply a logical extension of Fordism and the basic principles of Taylorism? Driving this debate is the larger issue of whether or not the interests of workers and management can be merged and harmonized (Hyman 1988). On one side of this debate are the "flexible specialization" theorists who envision a factory utopia in which the Japanese model will create a harmonious system of collaboration between management and workers. According to this scenario, workers willingly expand their responsibilities and increase their work loads by rotating jobs and revealing their hidden knowledge about work processes; in exchange for their collaboration, they get job security and more challenging work. At the other end of the debate, labor process theorists claim that the Japanese model is nothing more than an extension of Fordism (Dohse, Jurgens, and Malsch 1985). These analysts argue that the Japanese model or Toyotism has the same goal as Fordism but differs in its method of attaining that goal. Specifically, the Japanese model provides the means for resolving the problem of worker resistance to Taylorism (Dohse et al. 1985:128). They argue that the model's clever use of peer pressure as an instrument of control is a major factor underlying its advancement of management's agenda and for diffusing workers' resistance. Since the peer group has no collective means for resistance, management's agenda is less likely to encounter challenges and the scope of its directives becomes virtually unlimited (Dohse et al. 1985).

I concur with Dohse and his co-workers concerning the centrality of peer pressure as a means of control. Through peer pressure the model expands management's prerogatives and this helps explain why the model is so effective. However, I disagree with their other conclusions. First, the Japanese model has not solved the problem of worker resistance to Taylorism. Second, the model is not simply an extension of Fordism. It incorporates Taylorism but steps beyond Fordist principles to include social controls; in this respect, the Japanese model is post-Fordist.

In addition to the examples of peer pressure recounted in earlier chapters, during interviews with current workers I found that peer group pressure continues and may be intensifying through extensive use of temporary workers. One Associate interviewed told me:

Team work is not what it ought to be.
What do you mean?
We basically have two different teams. The last four processes are at the end. The four of them stick together. One of them has been caught several times allowing defects to go by.

Why?
Trying to get people in trouble.
Another guy is good. He's real fast, but he complains that we ought to fire them.
Who is "them"?
People who make mistakes. (Telephone interview, January 19, 1994)

The person quoted above had not read the manuscript. Another Associate, who had read it and to whom I told the story above about team members letting defects go by to get others into trouble, responded: "It is happening on the team before us. My team leader said when he was catching their mistakes: 'That team member is tired of fixing it so he's letting it go through' " (Interview, February 20, 1994).

Another aspect of peer pressure that I discovered in 1990 also continues. In chapter four I described a type of sexist peer pressure which had the effect of discouraging workers from reporting injuries because they feared being stigmatized. Injured workers were afraid others would believe that they were faking injury simply to get out of work (the Corporal Klinger syndrome). In 1994 an Associate said: "One girl on the team next to me wouldn't take the money they offered her if she would quit after she was injured. Now she is on IPC damage control [a job that is off the line and therefore very desirable]. Everyone resents her. Makes the ones that do get injured not say anything" (Telephone interview, February 20, 1994).

The preceding examples support the Fordist contention that the model uses peer pressure as a technique for disciplining the workforce. However, I believe that no matter how central peer pressure is to SIA's system of discipline, it does *not* discount the fact that the Japanese model represents something beyond Fordism.

In my view the debate misses the real issue. It is not necessary to believe that the model represents a step toward factory utopia in order to suggest that it represents something other than Fordism. Instead of discounting the effects of the Japanese model as merely a difference in method, I would argue that the issue *is* one of method because a company's goal is always the same—to maximize profits. The Japanese model is distinct from Fordism in that it is multidimensional and hegemonic in its methodology (its approach to control)—not because it is creating a democratic workplace.

To highlight the features of the Japanese model that make it a uniquely different system of control than what is found in Fordism, I will compare my experience at SIA to Ben Hamper's account in his book *Rivethead* (1986). He describes working as a "shop rat" at a GM assembly plant during the 1970s and 1980s. Conditions were similar to those I found concerning reactions to the Fordist, technical systems of control, particularly as regards the constant physical and mental drudgery of assembly line work. Hamper's accounts of wrestling certain parts again and again, the boredom of mindless repetition, and the way in which the minute hand on the clock scarcely seemed to budge immediately evoked my SIA work and similar feelings of frustration. I believe that this is part of a human being's natural reaction to the dehumanizing effects of Taylorism—to being turned into what seems like a machine. The natural physical and mental rhythm of working is gone. However, there are also important differences between Ben Hamper's shop rat experiences and those of an SIA Associate. I believe these differences are so significant as to warrant viewing the Japanese model as a post-Fordist system of control.

I found that the biggest difference between the work experience under the Japanese model as opposed to the traditional Fordist model occurred at an individual, psychological level. For example, I found it both confusing (as a worker) and interesting (as an observer) that the Japanese model creates a kind of psychological tension within the individual worker. This tension originates from desiring the improvements that the model brings to the traditional shop floor experience and, at the same time, resenting the fact that there is no avenue within the model for changing the performance requirement that comes with those improvements. The model's hegemonic approach has made it difficult to separate the good from the bad. The improvements are not minor. They include such things as a bright, clean, orderly work setting; a company culture that encourages supervisors to talk to you instead of yelling at you; and an environment that is supposed to celebrate the worker's role in production.

In the traditional Fordist model, as experienced by Ben Hamper's shop rats, this particular tension does not exist. Workers are free to hate their work openly. Their attitudes are their own. The bargain they strike with the company is simple and straightforward: make quota and you get your pay. Traditional Fordism did not interfere with the shop rat's personal autonomy. Workers' shop floor culture was a constant expression of individuality and a rejection of authority. Through their dress, music, language, and horseplay, shop rats created a distinct shop floor culture and their essential freedom remained intact. Ultimately, they beat the system by beating the clock through ingenious techniques of doubling up and creating spare time.

In Hamper's description of traditional Fordism, there is no expectation for workers to conform to some company standard of behavior or attitude. Individual autonomy was not under attack. In sharp contrast to that relative freedom of expression stands the Japanese model with its imposition of rigid conformity. The Japanese model creates a highly controlled atmosphere aimed at preventing workers from expressing their inherent resentment of authority and domination, which could potentially lead to concerted action and could foster their independence from company domination.

Although the Japanese model includes components of Fordism (e.g., assembly line production and technical innovation), it clearly steps beyond Fordism to impinge dramatically upon the social aspects of production. While Fordism ignores the social realm of production (and in doing so, allows for open expression by the individual worker), the hegemonic approach of the Japanese model incorporates Fordism's technical controls with cultural controls. The result is a system of social control driven by pressures for conformity to company goals. It attempts to harness a worker's total physical and mental attitude.

SIA clearly does not have the makings of a factory utopia. It is more accurately described as a factory driven by hidden intimidation—and open intimidation. The company's willingness to invoke sanctions is apparent in its communications and personnel practices. For example, SIA has sent a clear message that it may close its doors if workers try to organize:

> *Does the company talk about the union?*
> If there is a flier or a rumor of a meeting, the company shows
> a presentation on TV of all the GM plants that have closed
> [each team has a television set at its break area]. (Interview,
> January 24, 1994)

> *Do you think the workers will join a union?*
> People have never made this kind of money and they are
> scared the company will close the doors. (Telephone
> interview, January 20, 1994)

Beyond the ultimate threat of closure there are other structures of intimidation at work at SIA. The company has steadily built up an army of temporary workers or temps, hired from local agencies. SIA pays them lower wages and no benefits. In exchange, temps are given the opportunity to get a foot in the door and thus gain a chance at becoming one of the chosen few. Temps are part of the "other face" of the Japanese model: "The aim is to create a core of employees able to adapt to cyclical and secular changes in the level and composition of production. The central objective is to render workers disposable rather than adaptable. This is accomplished through subcontractors, temporary workers. . . . Flexibility thus entails intensified segmentation within the workforce between the relatively sheltered and advantaged and the vulnerable and oppressed" (Hyman 1988:56).

The effects of mixing an eager-to-be-exploited group of workers with a regular workforce should not be underestimated. What could provide a company with greater flexibility or control than institutionalizing a throwaway workforce? Temps are part of the psychological tension created by the Japanese model because they represent both a threat and a promise to the Associates. The following exchanges reveal SIA workers' awareness of the widespread use of temporary workers and the conflicting feelings Associates expressed concerning their use:

> *Tell me about the temporary workers. Have you worked with any? How are they treated?*
> There is one temp on my side. But probably one-third to one-half of the workforce on the whole is temps. There are more temps on second shift than on first. They are hiring some temps full-time now. Hired forty-three.
> *Do they still go through Orientation and Training?*
> Yes, they go two hours early for two weeks [two hours before the start of second shift]. They also have to go through the selection process and take all the tests. . . .
> *Any firings?*
> Lots of temps. (Interview, January 24, 1994)

> *What about temporaries?*
> I think over half our team is temps. They make about ten dollars per hour [According to this Associate, the wage rate was about $16.35 an hour for regular workers].
> *How many people are on your team?*
> Nine. (Interview, January 24, 1994)

> *Tell me about the temps, have you worked with any?*
> Oh yes, four out of ten on my team are temps.

How do you feel about the company using temporaries?
As long as they do it for the purpose of not laying me off, it's
great. There has been a shift in attitude about hiring. We were
important. The temps they hire as permanent learn as fast as
they can. They never take a day off. They can't say anything.
I think that this stays with them, because when they are hired
as permanent they still don't say anything. They have a mind
set. They still go through Training and Orientation, but it's
not the same. They hear all this good stuff [in Orientation and
Training classes], and you know, it's just a bunch of shit. It's
like when they brought those people who had already started
working and put them in our training class when we first
started.
How long do people work as temps?
I know one person who has been here almost two years as a
temp. He finally got hired as permanent. They still get ten
dollars an hour. One temp on my team is pretty slow. He's
between forty and forty-five. He tries hard not to push himself
over the limit. Everyone tries to help him out. (Telephone
interview, February 20, 1994)

The February 20 interview illustrates the psychological tension prevalent
in a workforce that is experiencing both the hidden discipline of peer
pressure and the reinforcing pressures of open intimidation through the
extensive use of temporary workers. It is apparent that this Associate is
relieved not to be among those suffering the pressures of constant job
insecurity. Even so, the Associate's comments indicate that the presence
of temps does create feelings of insecurity among permanent workers as
well. This is especially clear in the statement that the temps never take a
day off and keep their mouths shut. As the worker points out, the insecurity of temporary employment creates a mind set that stays with temps
even if they become Associates. Although the temps referred to by the
worker are now permanent Associates, the point is that they do not see
themselves as among the chosen few, which makes them a potential
threat to Associates.

The Purpose of the Japanese Model

Based on my findings, I believe that the purpose of the Japanese model
is not as its apologists declare: to involve workers in managerial decision

making in a factory utopia; rather, I view its purpose in exactly opposite terms. At SIA the Japanese model does not enhance workers' autonomy as regards policies and practices. It neither engages workers in managerial aspects of their jobs nor provides an avenue for real involvement in decision making. When workers did manage to have input into decisions affecting the quality of their lives, it was because they went outside the model's boundaries and approached the company as its adversary.

When I asked the workers I interviewed how much input they had in decisions that affected them, responses included "None" and "Never [was] asked." One Associate asked, "What do you mean?" "Like work policies," I suggested.

"None," was the answer. On the related issue of democratic input, I asked whether each interviewee's team had ever voted on anything. "Only on whether to have pizza," laughed one. "No," said a second. A third offered: "Only things like snacks of pizza. We did vote on that one job thing and someone took it out of our hands; the group leader on second shift vetoed it. He took on that authority. The "job thing" refers to an instance when the team had tried to change procedures at one of their stations but had been prevented from doing so.

On the surface the techniques of kaizening and decision making by consensus appear to enhance worker involvement and control. However, during my tenure at SIA, I found kaizening and consensus to be virtually appearance without substance. When I asked Associates in 1994 to talk about how kaizening is accomplished, their responses revealed the gap between ideals and realities:

> There are Star Dynamic meetings that started after you left, but they don't ever do nothing.

> Star meetings are only for bitches and gripes, to get it off their shoulders so they don't join the union.

> We kaizen things like making racks for parts. There are the Star Dynamics meetings. They cover five areas: quality, safety, materials. I can't remember the other two. They are like a regular morning meeting only on every other Wednesday from six-thirty to seven.

> All that stuff about kaizen and team concept, it's all just window dressing. (Various interviews, January–February, 1994)

The first two comments underscore the absence of substance, as does the third Associate's inability to recall the five basic areas of kaizening. The fourth person's comments neatly capture the widely shared cynicism among workers on the involvement issue. Repeated interview response patterns such as these call into question the idealized image of active worker involvement and commitment in such meetings. It must be pointed out that embracing an image of a progressive company that involves its workers in decision making is consistent with the hegemonic approach to control in the Japanese model. However, if the model actually did involve workers in decisions it would probably self-destruct because once given the opportunity, workers might take it well beyond its capacity to grant simple concessions.

Efforts to create an impression of involvement fulfill several objectives. At one level, such efforts create some converts among Associates, thereby encouraging division among workers and enhancing management prerogatives. At another level, the image of involved workers is aimed at the larger outside community, projecting the idea of a democratic company, a company the community can be proud of having attracted and clearly worth all of the tax monies and incentives used to bring it in. SIA's flat, decentralized management structure contributes an additional dimension to both the impression of worker autonomy and the company's community image. Yet, as we have seen, intense pressures to conform permeate this structure with team leaders and group leaders constantly monitoring each team member's behavior and performance. Hierarchy remains intact with top management directing team and group leaders, whose expectations are in turn quickly transferred to team members.

To summarize, the intent of this multidimensional, web-like structure is to create an inescapable, highly rationalized system of worker compliance. Compliance is gained indirectly as a worker identifies with teammates and internalizes the responsibilities of team membership. In turn, team membership creates a form of discipline that is either self-imposed or exerted by peers. If indirect measures fail, compliance can be directly enforced through the authority structure. Technical discipline reinforces social control with the computerized assembly line and just-in-time production setting the pace of work. Technical controls interconnect with indirect, social controls via the team structure where workers find themselves isolated within their independent teams from the rest of the plant. Ideologically, teams are unified through the company's common goal of profit making.

How Do Workers View the Model?

A recurring theme in workers' views of the Japanese model is the tension between their desire to realize the expectations that SIA would be a truly different place to work and the daily realities that cause those expectations to remain unfulfilled. The interviews illustrate a range of worker reactions to this tension. For some, hope remains that the model's promises of involvement and fulfillment can still be realized. For others, a sense of betrayal has replaced hope. Those who remain hopeful typically invoke explanations that blame various individuals for failure in implementing the model. These hopeful Associates represent a relatively low level of awareness of the potential gap between company and worker interests.

In the first example, a hopeful Associate blames group leaders for the tension, referring to the widespread optimism during start-up and identifying the reason for the change as the gap between Japanese and U.S. culture:

> *Have things changed?*
> It's not how it was when you were here. The work, policies,
> philosophy, it's all changed.
> *What do you mean?*
> The Japanese are much more into working for the good of the
> whole and we are more for number one. . . . The group leaders
> are basically brown nosers. If your team leader doesn't stand
> up to them and support the team, you are in bad shape.
> (Telephone interview, January 19, 1994)

According to another Associate who continues to have hopes for the Japanese model, it is not the Japanese or the model that present problems but the team and group leaders. This worker also attempts to separate the work experience from the model. For example, in reference to the manuscript, the Associate agrees with my negative assessments of work at SIA but believes that I was too negative about Japanese management, as though they were somehow separate from, instead of responsible for, the system of production:

> *Do you feel I'm way off base?*
> No, but you seemed negative. I didn't think it fair; the
> negative effects were the team leaders and group leaders. They
> didn't do their job right. They didn't buy into the quality first.
> You weren't being fair and were knocking Japanese
> management unfairly. But what you said about work was
> right.
> What the Japanese have done is they've hired from GM

and VW thinking they would take over. Might have been
better training them [group leaders] from the ground up and
teaching them the car business. There is a gap between those
really running the place and the executives.

I know someone who works in stamping and he said that
the Japanese would be shaking their heads about the quality
and the job of the group leaders. They use kanbon cards for
jobs. He also feels that the problem lies with the group leaders
and some team leaders and not the Japanese. (Telephone
interview, February 20, 1994)

This respondent brings up an interesting question: Would the model
work differently or meet the expectations of the workforce if the Japanese had hired management new to the auto industry, without the baggage of previous U.S. experiences? In my opinion it would not matter.
The outcome would not change substantially. In the end, the push for
profits is too great. It reaches beyond the individual.

The next two Associates describe working at SIA as a transforming
experience. They went in believing in one set of values and, as a result of
working at SIA, have since adopted a completely different set. One Associate changed from antiunion to prounion:

I was a totally antiunion person when I came here. My father-
in-law had worked at a Ford plant in another state. Ford
wanted concessions in benefits and he was against it. I said to
him, "What do you want, your benefits or your job?" and he
said, "By God, we had to fight for everything we got and I'm
not turning loose of them!" So I thought he was a jerk. I
believed that as long as I do my job and I work I don't need
no doggone union. It took me two or three months at SIA and
the injuries and the rate you had to work and I thought, there
is no way, not a shot in hell, that I can do this till I'm sixty-
five years old. They didn't have to hit me with a hammer to
wake me up. (Telephone interview, January 20, 1994)

Another Associate reveals an interesting gap that continues to prevail
between company and workers. The team spirit referred to below is not
company team spirit but reflects connectedness to one's work group. At
times, team members' sense of connectedness emerges in opposition to
the company which, in this example, is represented by the group leader:

Is there team spirit?
Yes, especially on my team. Also company wide. If you've got
a good team, that's the thing. The key is the team leader. A
good team leader defends the team against the group leader.
(Interview, January 20, 1994)

The previous two Associates' remarks represent how work realities can
lead to an emergent understanding of the gap between company and
worker interests, an understanding evident in identification with the team
(co-workers) needing to be defended against the company (group leader).

The next Associate also addresses the impact of the group leader.
Group leaders are the lowest-level salaried management employees;
therefore, they are the conduit for demands that the company places on
workers. This Associate does not make excuses for the system but sees it
as comparable to that in any other factory; a case of them versus us.
This worker's perspective represents a deeper understanding of the gap
between company and worker interests:

Is there team spirit?
Well, now that we got a new group leader it is better.
Associates don't really have much say, so if the company
wants to do something, they just do it. It's the same as the
place I used to work [previously did factory work]—the top
dogs run it. (Interview, January 24, 1994)

In their frustration, Associates are looking for someone to blame for
their disappointment, to ease the tension between expectations and reality. However, their expectations cannot be fully met by any group of
managers. Some may be friendlier than others and genuinely more caring,
but they have the same job to perform. The requirements of profit maximization do not change with the individuals performing the tasks.

Although the hopeful category of Associates includes a large number
of workers, my research indicates that the realities of work on the shop
floor generate a growing awareness among many workers of the futility
of the company's promises. Despite the model's idealized image and the
continuing hope of workers, two crucial dimensions of daily work experience are likely to increase the extent of critical understanding among
workers: intensification of work and related safety issues.

Work Intensification

As noted in chapter five, the pressures of team membership, when
combined with the computerized assembly line, kaizening, and just-in-

time production, create a constant, inescapable, fast work pace. In a typical U.S. auto plant, workers maintain a forty- to fifty-second-a-minute work pace, whereas Japanese auto plants tend to run close to sixty seconds a minute (Fucini and Fucini 1990:37). Another indication of how the model affects work pace is found in the amount of time spent assembling each car. In 1990, the average number of hours per assembled vehicle in U.S. plants was 25.1; in Japanese transplants it was 21.2; and for Japanese auto plants located in Japan the average was 16.8 hours (Womack, Jones, and Roos, 1990:92).

When discussing the current work pace, interviewees' responses reveal a condition of constant stress:

> *How have things changed?*
> Associate one: We don't have time to talk about anything anymore. Once they start that line, that's all you can think about.
>
> Associate two: If I was coming in now, I wouldn't make it two weeks. I've done enough to know I'm not going to cave—as long as I'm in the middle—not the fastest or the slowest. When I started, it was hard to get there because of go-go-go. You couldn't stop and begin to figure out how to do it easier. You gotta be fast. They are hiring younger, faster, and more competitive workers now.
>
> *What's a typical day like?*
> Associate three: The car line doesn't stop. We have the team meeting and then work all day. The line stops three minutes before the end of the shift, but we don't clean up. We did that when you were there. [The Associate is referring to the resistance that workers engaged in when the company took away our clean up period.]
>
> Associate four: No one pulls the cord. If the line stops it's because we run out of parts.
>
> Associate five: I'm work hardened now. But I'm sore every day. It's like I played football the day before. Another guy and I on my team worry because we are both over forty and what will happen when we can't keep up with the kids?
>
> *They are speeding the line up? How much?*
> Associate six: A tenth of a second. Sometimes they tell us about it, sometimes they don't. Takt time is continually

getting faster. They said they were cutting out eight seconds in the next couple of months.

I used to think it would be different. We're just busting our asses. My attitude has changed. Their main goal is making money. They want to make it more efficient. (Interviews, January–February, 1994)

Another traditional method of intensifying work is to lengthen the work day through overtime. At SIA, workers continue to have no say over the scheduling of overtime:

How does the company handle overtime?
Associate one: They tell you by the last break if you work over that day. By Thursday at end of the shift for Saturday. Or they can tell you: "we're working overtime" and then send you home. You never know how long you'll be there when you leave for work.

Associate two: Overtime has increased. Truck side is working nine-hour days and at least two Saturdays a month from here on out. I don't know what I would do if I had kids or any other responsibility. There is no time.

Associate three: Stress has really increased with overtime. Some can handle it and some can't. It shows up in your home life.
Why there?
Because that is where you have some leeway. You have none here. I absolutely thought it would be a family-oriented place. That's not the way it is, it's very different. It's not like that; you don't treat your family like they treat us. (Interviews, January–February, 1994)

Increasing the amount of work from a workforce by limiting the number of days available for vacation and time off is still another method of work intensification. SIA's practices in this area are apparent in what one Associate said: "Trying to get your vacation scheduled is like pulling teeth. No more than one person per team can be gone. I put in three requests and all three were turned down. A lot of workers just get paid for the time and never get to take their vacation days. It's by seniority. If you were hired in 1989, you get it. There is a shut-down in July of a week and you have to use three days plus two holidays" (Interview, January 20, 1994). These remarks also highlight tension stemming from the company's contradictory policy concerning seniority. At SIA seniority is used for certain issues, such as scheduling vacations, but not for others, such as job bidding or promotions.

Several responses to the question: "How long do you plan to work at SIA?" reveal that workers are beginning to realize the effects of work intensification. The responses also reflect the tension in the company's promise of lifetime employment:

> Associate one: I'd like to find another job that paid the same. I don't want to work there to retirement [laughter].
> *What makes you laugh?*
> The thought of doing what I'm doing at age sixty-five!

> Associate two: I'll be injured long before retirement.

> Associate three: Until they carry me out in a wheelbarrow. I used to work in a _____ and made nothing—with a boy at home that needed new shoes every six months.

> Associate four: Until I earn enough on my investments to retire, as long as I remain healthy. I get my fulfillment outside of work. (Interviews, January–February, 1994)

Safety

Perhaps the most volatile issue at SIA is safety. It is the single experience that most consistently causes workers to reexamine the company's intentions and that undermines the idealized image of the Japanese model. The extent of worker concerns involving injuries and the company's method of handling safety-related issues are illustrated by the following responses to questions regarding workers' safety and health (as before, all names used are false).

> *Any firings?*
> Associate one: Lots of temps. Also, injured workers have been followed and photos are taken of them. I know two incidents where workers were stalked. One was fired for lying on an

application. He didn't write down a previous injury and they called Wabash National where he had worked.

They fired a girl after ten days. She was in my training class. She was late once. They won't tell her why. But she filed a fair treatment card against the group leader.

What's a "fair treatment card"?

It's a card you can file if you feel someone is getting by with something—part of the fair treatment policy. You can request a peer review if you are fired. But no one has gotten their job back yet that I know of that went to peer review.

Associate two: Now one hundred percent wear safety glasses. There are monthly safety meetings and audits. There are more injured workers put on second shift. I think they are trying to get them to quit.

Associate three: What you said in the book, about the splints—I was in the supermarket line and the checkout person said to the woman in front of me (the woman had on wrist splints): "Oh, do you work at SIA? Seems like everybody out there wears them." But you don't see as many with splints like in the beginning because some are work hardened and then, like I told you before, the company has bought a lot of them off.

Do you remember Sally on the truck line? She was out for surgery on her wrists and elbows. She's back in the same group. They want to buy her out. [She is a single mother.]

Ever been injured?

Associate four: Yes, carpal tunnel. I was off three weeks. I'm still on the same job. The doctor said that if I didn't want permanent restriction then I had to go back to my job. [A permanent restriction often ended in job loss.]

Associate five: I was out for several months for injuries and the company is now trying to make me quit. They have put me on second shift now. They put me back to work twice without sending me to work hardening and my hand blew up.

Blew up?

It swells ungodly. The company doctor put me on five percent PDI (permanent disability) so I went to my family doctor and he sent me to a hand clinic. They told me that the problem was that the company never let me heal.

There are no sick days, only PTO [paid time off], two per year, plus ten days' vacation. The group leader must OK PTO. *Are they doing anything special for injured workers?* Only if you threaten with suing them. There are about twenty on first shift that have all been injured and now they work in IPD [in process damage]. They position people in different places to check for paint damage to trace where it is coming from.

What about Dr. _____, who was there in the beginning when I was? I thought he really cared about the workers. He was for the people. They railroaded him out. Any medical people that are for us they get rid of. They fired Sally Freed, and Debbie James—they fired her because she was for the people and she knew too much. She told me, she said: "Kathy, you been lied to. You were put back on those jobs because you could not do them because they want you out of there."

The fumes are terrible in paint. The paint dust and fumes. Only booth people have breathing protection. They call it the "paint plague." Some chemicals or something is causing it. People are getting nosebleeds and dry hacking coughs, also losing their voices. One girl lost hers for two days.

Associate six: You don't see the number of people in splints like we did when you were here. That's because how they handle injuries has changed. They do it three ways: One, people are bought off. Five thousand dollars and you are on your way. So you don't see them. Two, they have a work hardening program [physical training]. Three, there was an open period after you left when everyone could transfer, so people went to other jobs if they were injured at that time.

Associate one: We've been through five doctors since that first one. They can't keep them. *Why are they going through them so fast?* I think it is because in order for a person to get better they have to be taken off their job and that doesn't happen. They started a program to cut down on OSHA reportables. *How?* Made up some kind of rule on how things are recorded. They

called it guidelines to use for OSHA. (Interviews,
January–February, 1994)

Safety is a constant concern at SIA. Work intensification heightens
concerns with health and safety. Several quotes throughout this chapter
refer to staying healthy and remaining uninjured. As workers see inconsistencies between the company's expression of concern for employees
and the actual treatment of workers, a critical awareness of the gap between company and worker interests sharpens significantly.

Prospects for Unionization in Transplants

The prospects for unionizing transplants must be understood in the
context of the history and nature of company unions in the United States
and the role played by unions in Japan. Such unions illustrate how
worker organizations can approximate a regular union form but still be
devoid of real substance in terms of representing workers' interests.

An integral part of the American Plan (an employer antiunion
scheme—not limited to the auto industry—of the 1920s and 1930s) was
the creation of company unions to keep workers from forming their own
independent unions. Company unions are now illegal in the United States
because they violate national labor laws which were passed to protect a
worker's right to organize and promote workers' interests. A company
union is illegal because it succeeds in doing just the opposite. It is an
organization that is dominated by the company; therefore, instead of
workers' interests being represented, they are repressed.

In Japan, enterprise unions can be compared to company unions because they fulfill the same function. For example, the election of officers
is not held in secret but is witnessed by company officials; officers of
enterprise unions are often supervisory personnel; and union activity is
seen as a vehicle for moving up company ranks. In his analysis of Japanese industrial relations, Tokunaga describes the function of enterprise
unions: "Their principal function is to pursue management's interests,
not those of the union. To their minds, union activities are subordinate
to the interests of management. Thus, it is not unusual to find in some
cases that a union has become an important element of the enterprise's
management of the workforce and operates as a subsidiary to it"
(1983:321–22). Tokunaga cites one exception—enterprise unions are responsible for the policy of lifetime employment. He notes that the one

company practice enterprise unions have strongly resisted is the discharge of their members (1983:322). However, he qualifies the concept of lifetime employment in two ways: first, the lifetime employment system is for regular workers and depends upon a corps of part-time and seasonal workers; second, lifetime employment is only a tradition because there is no rule like the American seniority principle. Tokunaga adds that "of the regular employees, those most susceptible to discharge are older workers receiving relatively high wages" (1983:322).

A good portion of the success of the Japanese model within Japan arises from the fact that in enterprise unions, company interests predominate over worker concerns. Not only are enterprise unions weak forms of worker organization because they are company dominated but, just as important, such unions are limited in strength because they are company-based as opposed to industry-wide. A union structure based on the enterprise is simply not adequate to represent worker interests against the corporate interest of profit maximization. Because of its vulnerability, the enterprise union can be reduced to an additional component in management's control. In effect, the enterprise union becomes part of the web of corporate hegemony.

The United Auto Workers union, by contrast, has an industry-wide structure; therefore, it has the capacity to represent workers in ways that an enterprise union cannot. An examination of UAW experiences in its negotiations with car companies that use the Japanese model is in order. First is the case of NUMMI.

At NUMMI, Turner (1991) reports that for the most part workers like working in teams, giving input, job rotation, the clean environment, and the fact that they are treated with respect. However, he stresses that there continue to be traditional work-related problems that the union has yet to solve, such as out-sourcing jobs, limited training opportunities, short cycle time, high work standards, and pressure to avoid absenteeism. An additional concern that Turner warns against is the danger of the union losing its industrial identity and the possibility of an American version of enterprise unionism developing.

There seems to be a common tendency among many observers to believe that the union should have all of the answers and that changes should happen immediately. However, if this occurred, it would deny both the democratic process and the direct involvement of the rank and file. One must keep in mind that conditions are not changed overnight. At NUMMI, the union's democratic structure is working and changes are taking place at the rate at which the workforce is willing to invest the time and energy that such involvement requires. For example, by June of 1991 new local leadership had been elected at NUMMI. The new leaders pledged to fight more aggressively for greater control over line speed, for increased union independence, elimination of favoritism in assignments, and greater rank and file inclusion in decisions (Turner 1991). Once again, these changes will not take place overnight. Leaders are developing a solid foundation based on worker strength, a base that can be built upon and will hold up over time because the impulses arise from the workers themselves.

The UAW's impact on Saturn is also still evolving. The union is entering new territory in collective bargaining at Saturn by inserting itself into processes beyond the traditional union realm of "bread and butter" issues. It is capitalizing on the opportunities for involvement that the rhetoric of the Japanese model offers. For example, Wood stresses that already, management's rights are less clearcut (1988:112). Others report that workers are involved in higher level planning through manufacturing and strategic advisory committees (Kochan, Katz, and McKersie 1986:201).

Perhaps one of the more important issues for transplant workers, and particularly workers at SIA, is whether or not the union can aid in helping temporary workers become permanent employees. At Mazda, this is being addressed. According to Babson (1992), the union has narrowed the company's range of options for using temporary workers and has increased the opportunities for temps to become permanent employees. The goal is to prevent the company from using temps to avoid hiring regular full-time workers, as has clearly become the case at SIA, where temps are working two years and longer. In this way, the vulnerability of temps and their potential threat as replacements for regular workers can be done away with and temps will have almost as much to gain as do regular employees if workers choose to organize.

Before I speculate on the prospects for unionization at SIA, consider the responses of interviewees on the subject of unions:

Union?
Associate one: (solid union supporter): I'm pro.
Will workers organize a union?
Hard to tell.

Do you think the workers will join a union?
Associate two (transformed into union supporter at SIA):
People have never made this kind of money and they are

scared the company will close the doors. In 1991 SIA got hot
and heavy, with on-line TV—has updates and bulletins,
messages from VPs. SIA hired an antiunion firm. They use
scare tactics. The company said that if you sign a green card
to support a union election, they will find out, and by signing
the card it obligated the UAW to charge union dues—you
wouldn't sign a blank check, would you?

Will workers form a union?
Associate three: (uncommitted): Don't know.
Ever been approached about the union?
Yes. They pass out fliers at the plant gate. Workers stand by
the turnstiles and the company comes out and writes down
their badge numbers.

Do you think workers will organize?
Associate four: (antiunion): No. I'm against unions.
Have you been approached?
Yes.
How? What did you do?
They were leafleting at the gate about six months ago. I just
looked straight ahead and walked on. My husband is
prounion.
Does the company talk about the union?
Yes, they showed a film that told us we didn't have to sign a
card. That the union is an outside third party.

What do you think about a union?
Associate five (antiunion): I think SIA is doing things to avoid
getting a union in. Unions can be good when a company is
uncaring and to protect workers—health and safety and
workers' rights. But it's bad when it puts everyone on an
adversarial footing. It is a third party and the company may
not do something it would want to do because it has a union.
It is the International, not necessarily the Local that is the
problem.

But I'll vote for a union to protect my job, if it came to
that. For example, they changed the transfer policy. It used to
be that you put in a request of where you wanted to be and
when an opening came up, the first person that had put in the
request was chosen and locked in for one year. Now they post

openings so it is more competitive, there is no seniority. If
they would say to me because I am getting old: "You don't
seem to be doing too well," and try to get rid of me. As long
as the company is for the most part treating people fairly and
for those who don't have a tendency for repetitive motion
injuries, we're probably OK. (Interviews, January–February,
1994)

Associate five's remarks reveal more of the tension that workers experience at SIA. During the interview this worker had taken a clear anti-union stance. However, one can feel the uncertainty and fear in the Associate's answer. This worker is wondering if SIA is sincere concerning its promise of lifetime employment and is clearly uneasy about getting older in a plant that caters to young, healthy workers. Even though not supporting unions, the worker is beginning to express a favorable image of unions. The tension is evident when the Associate repeats the company's line that the union is a third party and attacks the International. This admonition directly follows a statement that unions protect workers and their rights.

The post-Fordist hegemonic approach of the Japanese model creates new challenges for U.S. unions. However, at the same time, I believe that it generates opportunities. It opens up a vast new territory in collective bargaining that has great potential for improving people's experience at work. The union's challenge lies in being able to separate the "bad" from the "good"—in untangling the tension created by the model. A key concept here is solidarity. In various ways the Japanese model inadvertently generates conditions which support the emergence of solidarity at its own expense.

No organizing drive can be truly successful unless the workforce internalizes, to some degree, the ageless concept of solidarity ("An injury to one is an injury to all"). Solidarity occurs as a person identifies his or her needs with the needs of others. It requires a certain level of caring and self-sacrifice. When workers act on these feelings, they build a network of trust. This trust is vital for holding workers together if a company exerts pressure and attempts to divide them. Solidarity is a source of psychological as well as organizational strength. At the psychological level, when other workers understand and confirm the beliefs of one worker, I know from experience, it is both uplifting and empowering. At the organizational level, worker solidarity exposes how the company's drive for profit maximization is in basic conflict with the interests of working people.

This research reveals that workers under the Japanese model expressed initial solidarity in the form of support for teammates in opposition to the group leader or company. Although identification with one's team and internalizing the responsibilities of team membership led to worker compliance with company demands, it often created a kind of protective or caring attitude toward teammates. It is my impression that the experience of working under the Japanese model and its team concept not only generates peer pressure; at the same time, it creates opportunities for workers to identify more easily with their work group, a traditional basis of worker solidarity.

In earlier chapters I argued that the Japanese model is unique because it attempts to manipulate workers' social experience within production. I believe that this is both the model's strength and its weakness. For the unskilled worker, gaining control over his or her life at work is accomplished through organizing around "social" issues. Traditionally, skilled workers have united around issues of protecting their skill and maintaining control over the technical aspects of their work. This is not possible for unskilled workers because they have no skill to protect. It is not their skill that the company wants but their total physical and emotional cooperation. One reason the Japanese model has been so successful in thwarting unionization is that it focuses on dominating the social aspects of production. It does so because that is exactly where workers turn in self-defense—they turn to each other. Therefore, it is only logical that the key to cracking the Japanese model is through a clear understanding of the power that is contained in workers' desire to improve their lot.

Factors that have traditionally unified unskilled workers have ranged from issues of simply figuring out ways of surviving the drudgery of assembly line work (as in Hamper's *Rivethead*) to gaining control over work pace and protecting themselves from the arbitrary actions of management. With the advent of the Japanese model, the union movement has been forced to consider the work experience in a broader context. Once traditional union goals are met, the structures found in the Japanese model provide openings for the union to begin focusing on the quality of the work experience itself. It can do so by involving the union more directly both in the process of production and in policy formulation.

Possibilities for Improvements

A key subset in the social dimension of the Japanese model is that the logic of the model is no longer based on the concept of the "family wage," as was true in Fordism. I believe that this opens up the possibility for emergence of new gender relations both at work and within the union movement. To indicate how this may be possible, I will examine the logic of Fordism and then contrast that with the thrust of post-Fordism.

According to Milkman, Ford's five-dollar-day wages (1914) laid the foundation for the auto industry to develop as a high-wage, capital-intensive industry which resulted in employers having little incentive to substitute cheap female labor for expensive male labor (1989:132). Ford referred to the wages he paid as a family wage and the man as a householder: "The man does the work in the shop, but his wife does the work in the home. The shop must pay them both" (Ford 1924:128). Not only did Ford receive tremendous support within the community for such a petition, but it also provided a new dimension of shop floor control which went beyond the technical control of the assembly line. Milkman explains how high wages became the supreme lever of control over the workforce:

> Mechanization was carried forward to such a great extent
> that wages became a relatively small component of costs. . . .
> In the major auto firms, the predominant policy was to pay
> high wages in exchange for subordination to the machine-
> paced organization of production. The combination of
> dramatically lowered turnover rates and the extra production
> extracted by means of the speed-up meant Ford workers
> produced more per dollar of wages after the implementation
> of the five-dollar day than before. Ford himself justifiably
> called it "one of the finest cost-cutting moves we ever made."
> (Milkman 1989:134)

As history has shown us, both of these methods of control have had long-lasting effects. High wages and capital intensification are hallmarks of manufacturing and the sexual division of labor that was established by such wage policy has persisted throughout the Fordist revolution. I believe that the Japanese model with its focus on the social aspects of production, shifting away from male-centered to team-centered work, provides an opening for the union to establish a new meaning for the term *family wage*. One of the distinctive features in work experience that I noted at SIA was that more often than not, women took the lead in criticizing the company and questioning its motives. Men were certainly involved but my point is that women experienced the intensification of work differently than did men because of their role in the family. In general, the burden of overtime is more intense for women because of their psychological as well as physical responsibilities in the home. Additionally, women in general are often the largest pool of low paid, temporary workers. They provide a huge untapped resource for organizing and because of their low wage stature, they represent the focus of future employment.

With a union particularly sensitive to these gender-related issues, workers have a chance of pushing the Japanese model beyond its present limitations and shaping it into something that more effectively reflects family/worker interests. However, as the Japanese experience has shown, only an industry-wide union, independent of company domination, has the capability to guide the company in a direction that forces it to make good on its rhetoric of worker involvement.

The Japanese model is not equipped to deliver on its promises to workers. During a corporation's quest to maximize profits, workers simply become expendable. Work intensification and safety, issues traditionally addressed by unions, are the first areas to be sacrificed for profit. However, although speedup and work injuries often provide the impetus for organizing, the only way an organizing drive can be successful at any of the transplants is if workers understand what is being done to them; if they do not forget what they have learned when the company attempts to improve conditions to keep workers from organizing; and if they are provided with outside support in resisting open intimidation during efforts to organize.

As the voices from the SIA shop floor reveal, some Associates continue to hope for a closer match between company rhetoric and work realities. Others have resigned themselves to viewing the company as comparable to more traditional employers or have begun to adopt explicitly adversarial views. Few SIA employees, however, have the time or energy required to analyze or penetrate the web of the company's social control. My hope is that this participant observer study may provide workers an alternative view of the work process and in so doing open up possibilities for transforming the workplace.

Bibliography

Adler, Paul S. 1993a. "Time-and-Motion Regained." *Harvard Business Review.* January–February: 97–108.

———. 1993b. "The 'Learning Bureaucracy': The United Motor Manufacturing, Inc." *Research in Organizational Behavior* (annual series). Greenwich, CT: JAI Press. Pp. 111–94.

Aronowitz, Stanley, 1973. *False Promises: The Shaping of American Working Class Consciousness.* New York: McGraw-Hill.

Babson, Steve. 1992. "Lean or Mean: The MIT Model and Lean Production at Mazda." Paper presented at Southern Political Science Association Annual Meeting, November 6, Atlanta.

———. 1993. "Whose Team? Lean Production at Mazda U.S.A." *Labor Studies Journal* 18, 2:3–24.

Berggren, Christian. 1992. *Alternatives to Lean Production: Work Organization in the Swedish Auto Industry.* Ithaca, N.Y.: ILR Press.

Berggren, Christian, Torsten Bjorkman, and Ernst Hollander. 1991. *Are They Unbeatable? Report from a Field Trip to Study Transplants, the Japanese Owned Auto Plants in North America.* Stockholm: Royal Institute of Technology.

Blauner, Robert. 1964. *Alienation and Freedom: The Factory Worker and His Industry.* Chicago: University of Chicago Press.

Boisot, Max. 1983. *Intangible Factors in Japanese Corporate Strategy.* Paris: Atlantic Institute for International Affairs.

Bollens, John, and Dale Marshall. 1973. *Guide to Participation.* Englewood Cliffs, N.J.: Prentice Hall.

Braverman, Harry. 1974. *Labor and Monopoly Capital.* New York: Monthly Review Press.

Brown, Clair, and Michael Reich. 1989. "When Does Union-Management Cooperation Work? A Look at NUMMI and GM–VanNuys." *California Management Review* Summer: 26–44.

Burawoy, Michael. 1979. *Manufacturing Consent: Changes in the Labour Process under Monopoly Capitalism.* Chicago: University of Chicago Press.

————. 1985. *The Politics of Production*. New York: Verso.

Cavendish, Ruth. 1982. *Women on the Line*. London: Routledge and Kegan Paul.

Chinoy, Ely. 1955. *The Automobile Workers and the American Dream*. Garden City, N.Y.: Doubleday.

Clarke, Simon. 1990. "The Crisis of Fordism or the Crisis of Social Democracy?" *Telos* 83:71–98.

Cole, Robert. 1979. *Work, Mobility and Participation: A Comparative Study of American and Japanese Industry*. Berkeley: University of California Press.

Cole, Robert, and Donald Deskins, Jr. 1988. "Racial Factor in Site Location and Employment Patterns of Japanese Auto Firms in America." *California Management Review* Fall: 9–22.

Derber, Charles, and William Schwartz. 1988. "Toward a Theory of Worker Participation." In Frank Hearn (ed.), *The Transformation of Industrial Organization*. Belmont, Calif.: Wadsworth.

Dohse, Knuth, Ulrich Jurgens, and Thomas Malsch. 1985. "From 'Fordism' to 'Toyotism'? The Social Organization of the Labor Process in the Japanese Automobile Industry." *Politics and Society* 14, 2:115–46.

Dore, Ronald. 1973. *British Factory—Japanese Factory: The Origins of National Diversity in Industrial Relations*. Berkeley: University of California Press.

Edwards, Richard. 1979. *Contested Terrain*. New York: Basic Books.

Fantasia, Rick, Dan Clawson, and Gregory Graham. 1988. "A Critical View of Worker Participation in American Industry." *Work and Occupations* 15:468–88.

Ferman, Louis, Michele Hoyman, Joel Cutcher-Gershenfeld, and Ernest J. Savoie (eds.). 1990. *New Developments in Worker Training*. Madison: University of Wisconsin, Industrial Relations Research Association.

Florida, Richard, and Martin Kenney. 1991. "Transplanted Organizations: The Transfer of Japanese Industrial Organization to the U.S." *American Sociological Review* 56:381–98.

Ford, Henry. 1924. *My Life and Work*. London: Heinemann.

Fucini, Joseph, and Suzy Fucini. 1990. *Working for the Japanese: Inside Mazda's American Auto Plant*. New York: Free Press, Macmillan.

Garrahan, Philip, and Paul Stewart. 1992. *The Nissan Enigma: Flexibility at Work in a Local Economy*. London: Mansell Publishing.

Gottfried, Heidi, and Laurie Graham. 1993. "Constructing Difference: The Making of Gendered Subcultures in a Japanese Automobile Transplant." *Sociology: The Journal of the British Sociological Association* 27:611–28.

Gottfried, Heidi, and Patricia Sotirin. 1991. "Research for Women: Notes toward the Development of a Liberatory Research Project." Unpublished paper.

Graham, Gregory. 1985. "Bureaucratic Capitalism and the Potential for Democratic Control." *Humanity and Society* 9:443–57.

Graham, Laurie. 1993. "Inside a Japanese Transplant: A Critical Perspective." *Work and Occupations* 20, 2 (May):147–73.

Grenier, Guillermo. 1988. *Inhumane Relations: Quality Circles and Anti-Unionism in American Industry*. Philadelphia: Temple University Press.

Hamper, Ben. 1986. *Rivethead: Tales from the Assembly Line.* New York: Time Warner.

Hill, Richard C., Michael Indegaard, and Kuniko Fujita. 1989. "Flat Rock, Home of Mazda: The Social Impact of a Japanese Company on an American Community." In Peter Arnesan (ed.), *The Auto Industry Ahead: Who's Driving?* Ann Arbor: University of Michigan, Center for Japanese Studies, Pp. 69–131.

Hodson, Randy, Sandy Welsh, Sabine Rieble, Cheryl Sorenson Jamison, and Sean Creighton. 1993. "Is Worker Solidarity Undermined by Autonomy and Participation? Patterns from the Ethnographic Literature." *American Sociological Review* 58 (June):398–416.

Hodson, Randy, Gregory Hooks, and Sabine Rieble. 1992. "Customized Training in the Workplace." *Work and Occupations* 19, 3 (August):272–92.

Hodson, Randy, and Teresa Sullivan. 1990. *The Social Organization of Work.* Belmont, Calif.: Wadsworth.

Howes, Candace. 1992. *Foreign Direct Investment in the Auto Industry.* University of Notre Dame: Department of Economics.

Hull, Frank, and Koya Azumi. 1988. "Technology and Participation in Japanese Factories: The Consequences for Morale and Productivity." *Work and Occupations* 15, 4 (November):423–48.

Hyman, Richard. 1988. "Flexible Specialization: Miracle or Myth?" In Richard Hyman and Wolfgang Streeck (eds.), *New Technology and Industrial Relations.* Oxford: Basil Blackwell. Pp. 48–60.

International Metalworkers Federation. 1992. *Toyota Motors towards 2000: A Report for Workers and Their Unions.* Toyota City, Japan: Toyota World Auto Council, May 27–29.

Jarrett, Paula. 1993. "SIA Sued for Racism: Ex-worker Wants Job Back." *Journal and Courier,* Lafayette, Indiana, July 22, p. 1.

Jurgens, Ulrich. 1993. "Lean Production in Japan: Myth and Reality." In Wolfgang Littek and Toni Charles (eds.), *The New Division of Labour.* Berlin and New York: De Gruyter.

Kamata, Satoshi. 1982. *Japan in the Passing Lane.* New York: Pantheon Books.

Katz, Harry. 1985. *Shifting Gears: Changing Labor Relations in the U.S. Automobile Industry.* Cambridge, Mass.: MIT Press.

Kenney, Martin, and Richard Florida. 1988. "Beyond Mass Production: Production and the Labor Process in Japan." *Politics and Society* 16, 1:121–58.

———. 1993. *Beyond Mass Production: The Japanese System and Its Transfer to the U.S.* New York: Oxford University Press.

Klug, Thomas. 1989. "Employers' Strategies in the Detroit Labor Market, 1900–1929." In Nelson Lichtenstein and Stephen Meyer (eds.), *On the Line: Essays in the History of Auto Work.* Urbana: University of Illinois Press. Pp. 42–72.

Knights, David, and David Collinson. 1985. "Redesigning Work on the Shopfloor: A Question of Control or Consent." In David Knights, Hugh Willmott, and David Collinson (eds.), *Job Redesign: Critical Perspectives on the Labor Process.* Aldershot, England: Gower. Pp. 197–226.

Kochan, Thomas, Harry Katz, and Robert McKersie. 1986. *The Transformation of American Industrial Relations.* New York: Basic Books. Reprint, Ithaca, N.Y.: ILR Press, 1994.

Kornbluh, Hy. 1984. "Work Place Democracy and Quality of Work Life: Problems and Prospects." *Annals of the American Academy of Political and Social Science* 473 (May):88–95.

Lawler, Edward. 1986. *High-Involvement Management: Participative Strategies for Improving Organizational Performance.* San Francisco: Jossey-Bass Publishers.

Lincoln, James, and Arne Kalleberg. 1985. "Work Organizations and Work Force Commitment: A Study of Plants and Employment in the U.S. and Japan." *American Sociological Review* 50 (December): 738–60.

Linhart, Robert. 1981. *The Assembly Line.* Amherst: University of Massachusetts Press.

Marx, Jonathan. 1988. "Organizational Recruitment as a Two-Stage Process: A Comparative Analysis of Detroit and Yokohama." *Work and Occupations* 15, 3:276–93.

Milkman, Ruth. 1989. "Rosie the Riveter Revisited: Management's Postwar Purge of Women Automobile Workers." In Nelson Lichtenstein and Stephen Meyer (eds.), *On the Line: Essays in the History of Auto Work.* Urbana: University of Illinois Press. Pp. 129–52.

———. 1991a. *Japan's California Factories: Labor Relations and Economic Globalization.* Los Angeles: University of California, Institute of Industrial Relations.

———. 1991b. "Labor and Management in Uncertain Times: Renegotiating the Social Contract." In Alan Wolfe (ed.), *America at Century's End.* Berkeley: University of California Press. Pp. 131–51.

Molstad, Clark. 1988. "Control Strategies Used by Industrial Brewery Workers: Work Avoidance, Impression Management and Solidarity." *Human Organization* 47, 4:354–60.

Parker, Mike. 1985. *Inside the Circle: A Union Guide to QWL.* Boston: South End.

Parker, Mike, and Jane Slaughter. 1988. *Choosing Sides: Unions and the Team Concept.* Boston: South End.

Perrucci, Robert. 1994. *Japanese Auto Transplants in the Heartland.* Hawthorne, N.Y.: Aldine de Gruyter.

Pfeffer, Richard. 1979. *Working for Capitalism.* New York: Columbia University Press.

Piore, Michael, and Charles Sabel. 1984. *The Second Industrial Divide.* New York: Basic Books.

Robertson, David, James Rinehart, Christopher Huxley, Jeff Wareham, Herman Rosenfeld, Alan McGough, and Steve Benedict. 1993. "Japanese Production Management in a Unionized Auto Plant." Willowdale, Ontario: Canadian Automobile Workers (CAW)–Canada Research Department.

Roy, Donald. 1960. " 'Banana Time': Job Satisfaction and Informal Interaction." *Human Organization* 18, 4:158–68.

Rubinstein, Saul, Michael Bennett, and Thomas Kochan. 1993. "The Saturn Partnership: Co-Management and the Reinvention of the Local Union." In Bruce E. Kaufman and Morris M. Kleiner (eds.), *Employee Representation: Alternatives and Future Directions.* Madison: University of Wisconsin, Industrial Relations Research Association. Pp. 339–70.

Safizadeh, M. Hossein. 1991. "The Case of Workgroups in Manufacturing Operations." *California Management Review* Summer:61–82.

Schattschneider, Elmer Eric. 1960. *The Semi-Sovereign People.* New York: Holt, Rinehart, and Winston.

Slaughter, Jane. 1983. *Concessions and How to Beat Them.* Detroit: Labor Education and Research Project.

Subaru-Isuzu Automotive Inc. 1989. "Deming Handout"

Subaru-Isuzu Automotive Inc. 1989. "Nanatsu—No Muda: 7 Wastes"

Subaru-Isuzu Automotive, Inc.: Facts and Information. 1989. Produced in cooperation with Indiana Department of Employment and Training Services.

Subaru-Isuzu Automotive Inc. 1989. *SIA Associate Handbook.* August (first edition).

Tausky, Curt, and Anthony Chelte. 1991. "Employee Involvement: A Comment to Grenier and Hogler." *Work and Occupations* 18, 3 (August):334–42.

Taylor, Frederic. 1911. *The Principles of Scientific Management.* New York: Harper.

Thomas, Robert J. 1985. "Quality and Quantity: Worker Participation in the U.S. and Japanese Automobile Industries." In Melvyn Dubofsky (ed.), *Technological Change and Workers' Movements.* Beverly Hills, Calif.: Sage. Pp. 162–88.

Thompson, Paul. 1989. *The Nature of Work: An Introduction to Debates on the Labour Process,* 2d edition. Atlantic Highlands, N.J.: Humanities Press International.

Tokunaga, Shigeyoshi. 1983. "A Marxist Interpretation of Japanese Industrial Relations, with Special Reference to Large Private Enterprises." In Taishire Shirai (ed.), *Contemporary Industrial Relations in Japan.* Madison: University of Wisconsin Press. Pp. 313–30.

Turner, Lowell. 1991. *Democracy at Work: Changing World Markets and the Future of Labor Unions.* Ithaca, N.Y.: Cornell University Press.

Van Maanen, John. 1977. "Experiencing Organization." In John van Maanen (ed.), *Organizational Careers: Some New Perspectives.* New York: Wiley. Pp. 15–45.

Whyte, William Foote. 1984. *Learning from the Field: A Guide from Experience.* Beverly Hills, Calif.: Sage.

Womack, James, Daniel Jones, and Daniel Roos. 1990. *The Machine That Changed the World.* New York: Rawson Associates.

Wood, Stephen. 1988. "Between Fordism and Flexibility? The US Car Industry." In Richard Hyman and Wolfgang Streeck (eds.), *New Technology and Industrial Relations.* Oxford: Basil Blackwell.

Woronoff, Jon. 1981. *Japan's Wasted Workers.* Toyowa, N.J.: Allenheld.

Zahavi, Gerald. 1983. "Negotiated Loyalty: Welfare Capitalism and the Shoeworkers of Endicott Johnson, 1920–1940." *Journal of American History* 70: 602–20.

Zwerdling, Daniel. 1980. *Workplace Democracy.* New York: Harper Colophon.

Index

Adler, Paul S., 10, 11
African Americans, racial discrimination and, 67–68
Agitation, organized, 125–27
American Plan, 147
Anonymous letters, resistance through, 117, 120–21
Anti-Japanese sentiment, 57–58
Anti-union sentiment
  company, 12–13, 22, 30, 57, 134, 147, 150
    American plan, 147
  worker, 42–43, 150–51
Assembly line, 62
  computerized, 112–14, 115
  steps in, 71–76
    Body department, 73
    Paint department, 73–74
    Stamping department, 73
    Trim and Final, 74–76
  tasks and problems on, 76–85
  worker response to, 117
Associates, 48, 64
  use of term, 20, 85, 107
Attitude questionnaire, 22–23
Attitudes, pre-employment selection and workers', 35
Authority, compliance through direct, 101–4
Automation, 73. *See also* Assembly line

Autonomy, worker, 2, 138
  Japanese model and, 137
  personal or individual, 133–34
  UAW's partnership structure of governance and, 13

Babson, Steve, 12, 149
Behavior training, 46–50
Benedict, Steve, 9
Bennett, Michael, 13
Berggren, Christian, 18, 86–87
Beyond Mass Production: The Japanese System and Its Transfer to the U.S. (Kenney and Florida), 7
Bias, mobilization of, 34
Bjorkman, Torsten, 18, 86–87
Blacks, racial discrimination against, 67–68
Body department, 73
Break time, 70–71
Brown, Clair, 11
Burawoy, Michael, 97, 106
Bureaucracy, learning, 10

CAMI Automotive, 9
Canada, transplants in, 9
Capital intensification, 153
Carpal tunnel syndrome, 65, 86, 87–90, 145
  stigma attached to, 91–92

Ceremonies, and sense of belonging, 110–12
Chain of command, 48
Chassis work area, 75
"Check-man" points, 75–76
Chinoy, Ely, 16
Chrysler, Product Quality Improvement at, 6
Circuit board exercise, 23–24
Class distinctions, blurring of, 53
Cleanup, 78, 120, 122–23
Collective bargaining, 9, 149, 151
Collective resistance, 117–18, 121–27, 128
Commitment, 93, 95, 98, 138
Communication
    top-down policy making, 59, 121–25
    training ideals vs. work realities, 59–60, 126–27
Company philosophy, SIA, 45–46, 94–96, 100
    American traditions and, 95
    shop floor reality vs., 58–61, 85–93, 126–27, 141
Company unions, 147–48
Compliance
    through direct authority, 101–4
    as goal, 97, 138
    through mutual support, 101
    through peer pressure, 99–101, 114, 131–32
    through self-discipline, 98–99
    during training, 56–57
    worker selection process and, 33–35
Computerized assembly line, 112–14, 115
Conformity, 58, 134, 138. *See also* Control, bases of
Consensus in decision making, 106, 137–38
Continuous improvement, 10, 11. *See also* Kaizen
Contract workers, 85
Control, bases of, 94–115. *See also* Orientation and Training; Pre-employment screening; Shop floor control; Worker control

hegemonic, 97, 98–104, 132, 133, 134, 138
multidimensional, 97–98, 115, 132
social control, 19, 98–112, 131, 134, 138, 152, 154
    culture of cooperation through egalitarian symbols, 106–12, 114
    kaizen philosophy, 104–6, 114
    team concept, 98–104
technical control, 112–15, 138
    computerized assembly line, 112–14, 115
    just-in-time production, 77–78, 114–15
Conveyer systems, overhead, 74–75
Cooperation
    between associates, emphasis on, 20–21
    culture of, through egalitarian symbols, 106–12, 114
    to humiliate team member, 100–101
    labor-management, Japanese model and, 1–2
Corporate character, 108
Corporate culture, 60, 96
Cross-Cultural Training, 48–50
Cultural control, 106–12
Culture
    of cooperation, 106–12, 114
    corporate, 60, 96
    shop floor, 106–7, 133–34

Decision making
    consensus in, 106, 137–38
    team, 57
Defect report sheet, 118
Deming, W. Edward, 51
Deming management method, 51–52
"Deming's Seven Deadly Diseases," 52
Democracy in workplace, 9, 102, 137
Department managers, 48, 64
Department meetings, 112
    organized agitation at, 125–27
Department of Employment and Training (DET), Indiana, 20
Deskilling, 7

Despotic control, 97
Direct authority, compliance through, 101–4
"Direct runners," 76
Direct technical control, 112–14
Discipline among teams, diversity in, 102–3, 104. *See also* Compliance
Discrimination
  racial, 67–68
  sexual, 66
Division of labor
  racial, 67–68
  sexual, 65–67, 153
Doctors, company, 146
Dohse, Knuth, 11, 131
Double standards, 41, 119–20
"Driving out fear," 107
Drug use, and double standard, 41

Economic discipline, 10
Egalitarianism
  and culture of cooperation, 106–12, 114
  office arrangement and, 48–49
  shop floor reality and, 85–86
Employee Involvement (EI) program at Ford, 6
Empowerment, solidarity and worker, 151
Enterprise unions, 147–48
Exercise routine
  resistance to, 68–69, 120, 121
Expectations vs. work reality, 7–8, 12, 58–61, 138–41

Factory utopia, 3, 131
Fair treatment card, 145
Fair treatment policy, 120
Falling behind on the line, 78
Family environment, encouragement of, 54, 58
Family wage, 152–53
Final line, 75
Firings, 144–45, 146
Flat management structure, 47–48, 64, 138

Flexibility, temporary workers and, 135–36
Flexible specialization, 131
Florida, Richard, 7–8
Fordism, 1, 131, 132
  logic of, 153
  traditional, 133–34
Ford Motor Company, 6, 12
Friendships among workers, 37, 61
Fucini, Joseph, 3, 12, 32
Fucini, Suzy, 3, 12, 32
Fuji Heavy, 44
Fujita, Kuniko, 18

Garrahan, Philip, 8
General Aptitude Test (GAT), 20, 21
General Motors, 44, 50
  joint ventures, 6, 9–11
  Linden plant, 6–7
  Lordstown (Ohio) plant, 4–5
  QWL, 5
  Saturn plant, 13
Grand opening celebration, 111
Group leaders, 108
  in SIA organizational structure, 48, 64
  team spirit and, 141
  workers' view of, 139–40

Hamper, Ben, 133–34
Hand injuries, 86–93
Hangers, 74
Hazardous materials
  disposal of, 54
  and "right to know" law, 127
Health issues, collective resistance over, 127. *See also* Injuries; Safety
Hegemonic control, 97, 132, 133, 134, 138
  team as driving structure behind, 98–104
Hierarchy, 10. *See also* Flat management structure
Hill, Richard C., 18
Hiring process. *See* Pre-employment screening

Hodson, Randy, 36, 37
Hollander, Ernst, 18, 86–87
Honda
    injuries, 86–87
    U.S. assembly plants, 6
Hooks, Gregory, 36, 37
Housekeeping, 78, 120, 122–23
Huddle ritual, 69–70, 110, 121
Humanization of work, 5, 10
Human relations, blending with tech-
    nological improvements, 2
Humor, and resistance, 121
Huxley, Christopher, 9

Identification with team, 98, 152
Indegaard, Michael, 18
Indiana site, 44–45
Individual resistance, 117, 118–21,
    127
Injuries, 62
    firing workers with, 144–45
    line speed and, 71
    peer pressure over reporting, 132
    repetitive-motion, 86–93
    shop floor reality vs. company phi-
        losophy regarding, 86–93
    "trigger finger," 92
    unofficial kaizen to prevent, 82–83
    workers' views of, 145–47
    wrist and hand, 84–93
        carpal tunnel syndrome, 65, 86,
            87–92, 145
Innovation-Mediated Production, 7
Inspections on assembly line, 75–76
Instructors, training, 41, 54–55, 61
Intensification, work. *See* Work inten-
    sification
"Interaction" program, 47
Internalization of team membership,
    98–99
International Metalworkers Federa-
    tion, 3
Interpersonal skills, 18
Interviews, screening, 28–29
Intimidation, company use of, 124,
    134–36

Inventory control, just-in-time system
    of, 77–78, 114–15
Isuzu, history of, 44

Japan, unions in, 147–48
Japanese model
    debate over, 1–4, 130–36
    Fordist model vs., 1, 131, 132, 133–
        34, 153
    industry analysis and, 7–9
    and influence in United States, 1
    possibilities for improvements of,
        152–54
    as post-Fordist system of control, 3,
        131–36, 151
    purpose of, 136–38
    SIA study, background and methods
        used in, 13–17
    success of, within Japan, 148
    tensions regarding, 57–58
    UAW experiences at companies
        using, 148–49
    U.S. experiments with, 4–7
    U.S. transplant studies and, 8, 9–13
        Mazda, 11–13
        NUMMI, 9–11, 12
        Saturn, 13
    workers' views of, 138–47
        safety and, 144–47
        work intensification and, 141–44
Japanese workers as model, 55–56
Job enrichment movement, 5
Job redesign movement, 4–5
Job satisfaction, worker participation
    and, 96–97
Job security, 94
Joint ventures, 6, 9–11
Jokes, and resistance, 121
Jones, Daniel, 3–4, 7
Jurgens, Ulrich, 11, 131
Just-in-time production, 77–78,
    114–15

Kaizen, 20
    domino effect on workforce, 105–6
    jokes about, 121

philosophy of
Deming and, 51
social control through, 104–6,
114
training ideals vs. work realities regarding, 59
unofficial, 82–83
workers' perspectives on, 137–38
Kaizen Wheel, 45–46
Kamata, Satoshi, 11, 104
Kenney, Martin, 7–8
Kochan, Thomas, 13
KPs (key principles), 47

Language, and culture of cooperation,
107–10
Lawler, Edward, 5
Lean production, 1, 3, 4. *See also* Japa-
nese model
Learning, general areas of, 43–50
Learning bureaucracy, 10
Learning Enhancement course, 50
Lifetime employment, 144, 147–48,
151
Line stoppages, 78–79, 85, 112, 113,
125
Logo, company, 44

McGough, Alan, 9
*Machine That Changed the World,
The* (Womack et al.), 7
Making out, 106. *See also* Kaizen
Malsch, Thomas, 11, 131
Management, philosophy of, 51–54,
94
ten principles of, 53
Management control. *See* Control,
bases of
Management structure, flat, 47–48,
64, 138
Manufacturing Task exercise, 25–26
Material handlers, 77–78
Mazda Motor Manufacturing (USA)
Corporation, 11–13
pre-employment screening at, 18
UAW and use of temps at, 149
worker injuries at, 86

Milkman, Ruth, 6–7, 12–13, 153
Mind set of temporary workers, 136
Mobilization of bias, 34
Morning team meeting, 69
organized agitation at, 125–27
resistance during, 118, 119
Motivation
competition with Japanese worker
model as, 55–56
pre-employment screening and, 31–
32, 34
worker control and, 10
Multidimensional control, 97–98,
115, 132. *See* Control, bases of
Mutual support, compliance through,
101

National Quality of Work Life Com-
mittee, 5
New United Motors Manufacturing
Inc. (NUMMI), 6, 12, 96
studies of, 9–11
UAW at, 148–49
Nissan
organizing campaign, 9
Sunderland (England) plant, 8
union vote, 57, 58
U.S. assembly plants, 6
Noise level, 71
NUMMI. *See* New United Motors
Manufacturing Inc. (NUMMI)

On-line repair, 76
Operating Committee, 47–48, 64
Operating principles, 53, 126
Operation Instruction Sheets, 55
Organizing campaign, Nissan, 9
Orientation and Training, 36–61
expectations based on, 7–8
general areas of learning in, 43–50
schedule of, 37–39
socialization during, 36–37
technical training, 36, 50–61
ideals vs. work realities, 58–61
OSHA reportables, 146–47
Overhead conveyer systems, 74–75

Overtime, 11, 154
  scheduling of, 123–25, 143
"Overwork syndrome," 86. *See also*
    Injuries

Paid time off (PTO), 146
Paint department, 73–74
Parker, Mike, 3, 96
Participant observation method, 13,
    15–17
Partnership structure of governance at
    Saturn, 13
Parts shortages, 77–78
Peer pressure, compliance through,
    99–101, 114, 131–32
Philosophy
  company, 45–46, 94–96, 100
    American traditions and, 95
    shop floor reality vs., 58–61, 85–
      93, 126–27, 141
    of management, 51–54, 94
    quality, 52
Physical exam, 27–28
Plant layout, 63
Post-Fordism, 3, 131–36, 151
Pre-employment screening, 18–35
  focus of U.S. vs. Japanese, 18–19
  as gatekeeper, 19, 30, 32, 33
  interpersonal skills and, 18
  at NUMMI, 11
  and selection process, 20–29
    interviews, 28–29
    Phase I, 22–25
    Phase II, 25–27
    physical exam, 27–28
    worker response, 19, 29–33
  theoretical implications of, 33–35
Pride, team, 100–101
Profit maximization, 98, 138, 141,
    148, 154
Protest, silent, 117, 120

Quality circles, 5
Quality of Work Life (QWL) pro-
    grams, 5
Quality philosophy, SIA, 52

Racial discrimination, 67–68
Racial division of labor, 67–68
Recruitment. *See* Pre-employment
    screening
Red cord line stop, 79
Reich, Michael, 11
Repair, on-line, 76
Repetitive-motion injuries, 86–93
  carpal tunnel syndrome, 65, 86, 87–
    92, 145
Resistance
  bases of, 116–28
    collective resistance, 117–18,
      121–27, 128
    individual resistance, 117, 118–
      21, 127
    worker selection process, 33–35
  to exercise routine, 68–69, 120, 121
  multidimensional control and, 98
Responsibilities of team membership,
    internalization of, 98–99, 152
Rieble, Sabine, 36, 37
"Right to know" law concerning haz-
    ardous materials, 127
Rinehart, James, 9
Rituals, 69–70
  to create sense of belonging, 110–12
  resistance to, 117, 118–19, 121
Rivethead (Hamper), 133–34
Robertson, David, 9
Robots, subassemblies done by, 73
Roos, Daniel, 3–4, 7
Rosenfeld, Herman, 9
Rubinstein, Saul, 13

Sabotage, 125
Safety. *See also* Injuries
  collective resistance over, 127
  company emphasis on, 45
  workers' view of, 144–47
  work process and, 93
Safety representatives, 59
Saturn, 6, 13, 149
Scheduling
  of overtime, 123–25, 143
  of vacation, 143–44

Selection, worker. *See* Pre-employment screening
Self-discipline, compliance through, 98–99
Seniority, 144
Sexual discrimination, 66
Sexual division of labor, 65–67, 153
Sexual harassment, 41, 91–92
Shift rotation, 59–60
  organized agitation over, 125–27
Shop floor control
  high wages of Fordism and, 153
  Orientation and Training for, 61
  pre-employment screening and, 33–34
Shop floor culture, 133–34
  shaped through team structure, 106–7
Shop floor reality vs. company philosophy, 58–61, 85–93, 126–27, 141
SIA. *See* Subaru-Isuzu Automotive (SIA)
SIA Associate Handbook, 85, 108
  company philosophy from, 94–96
Sick days, 146
Signs, culture of cooperation through, 108–10
Sketching, 52
Slaughter, Jane, 3, 96
Sleep disturbances, 15
Slogans, use of, 108–10
Social control, 19, 98–112, 131, 134, 138, 152, 154
  culture of cooperation through egalitarian symbols, 106–12, 114
  kaizen philosophy and, 104–6, 114
  team concept and, 98–104
Socialization
  in Orientation and Training, 36–37
  pre-employment screening and, 33–34
Solidarity, Japanese model of, 151–52
Specialization, flexible, 131
Speedup, 11, 62
  injuries and, 71, 86–93
  just-in-time production and, 114

kaizening enforced through, 105–6
  team culture and support of, 107
  time and motion studies and, 55
  workers' views of, 57, 142–43
Splints, use of, 89–90, 91, 145
Staff Associates, 48, 54
Stamping department, 73
Star Dynamic meetings, 137
Start-up period, 117
  studying SIA during, 15–16
Statistical Process Control (SPC), 51
Statistical Quality Control, 6
Stereotypes, 48–49
Stewart, Paul, 8
Stress
  injuries and, 86–93
  work intensification and, 142–43
Subaru-Isuzu Automotive (SIA)
  background and methods used in study of, 13–17
  company philosophy of. *See* Company philosophy, SIA
  history of, 44–45
  management philosophy of, 51–54, 94
  organizational structure of, 47–48, 64, 138
  quality philosophy of, 52
Swedish auto industry, 7
Symbolic rituals, 110–12

Takt time, 75, 79, 105, 143
Taylorism, 7, 8, 131, 133
Team concept, 94
  emphasis on, 20–21, 32, 53–54
  shaping workers' culture through, 106–7, 108
  social control through, 98–104
  training ideals vs. work realities regarding, 58–59, 60
  worker solidarity based on, 152
Team decision making, 57
Team exercises in pre-employment screening, 23–25, 27
Team leaders, 108
  compliance through direct authority of, 101–4

confrontations with, 119
and frustration about position,
103–4
and pressure not to stop line, 77
role of, at Mazda, 12
in SIA organizational structure, 48,
64
workers' view of, 139–40
Team leader training, 66–67, 99, 100
Team pride, 100–101
Team spirit, 9, 140–41
Technical control, 112–15, 138
computerized assembly line, 112–
14, 115
just-in-time production, 77–78,
114–15
Technological changes, and work, 6–7
Temporary workers, 85–86, 144
Associates' views of, 131–32,
135–36
exploitation of, 11, 12, 35
unions and, 149
women as, 154
Testing, pre-employment, 20–27
Time and motion studies, 10, 55
kaizening and, 105–6
Time off, 143–44
Token card, 73
Tokunaga, Shigeyoshi, 147–48
Toyota, 11
joint ventures, 9–11
pre-employment screening, 18
union avoidance strategy, 3
U.S. assembly plants, 6
Toyotism, 131. *See also* Japanese
model
Training, 50–61
behavior, 46–50
Cross-Cultural, 48–50
ideals of, vs. work realities, 58–61
team leader, 66–67, 99, 100
U.S. vs. Japanese, 36
Training instructors, 41, 54–55, 61
Transplants, 8–13
prospects for unionization in, 147–
52, 154
studies of, 9–13

unionized, 8–9
unorganized, 9
Trim and Final department, 74–76
Turner, Lowell, 10–11, 148–49

Unemployment, "world view" of
NUMMI workers due to, 10
Unions
anti-union sentiment
American plan, 147
of company, 12–13, 22, 30, 57,
134, 147, 150
of workers, 42–43, 140, 150–51
company, 147–48
enterprise, in Japan, 147–48
Nissan organizing campaign, 9
prounion sentiment, 140
transplants, 8–9
prospects for unionization, 147–
52, 154
worker participation, 2–3
workers' views, 149–51
United Automobile Workers (UAW),
5–6, 12, 13, 148–49
U-turn, 65

Vacation scheduling, 143–44

Wage, 64
family, 152–53
of temps, 86
Wareham, Jeff, 9
Waste, training handout on, 46
Womack, James, 3–4, 7
Women
sexual division of labor and, 65–67,
153
sexual harassment and, 41, 91–92
work intensification experience for,
153–54
Wood, Stephen, 6, 149
Work, seven principles of, 46
Worker compliance. *See* Compliance
Worker control, 2
motivation and, 10
Worker participation, 2–3, 95–97
efforts to create impression of, 138

job satisfaction and, 96–97
at NUMMI, 10
resistance through refusal of, 117–19
U.S. historical roots of, 4–7
Worker resistance. *See* Resistance
Worker selection. *See* Pre-employment screening
Working class life, 97
Work intensification, 62, 104, 105–6. *See also* Assembly line; Just-in-time production
health and safety concerns and, 147
women's experience of, 153–54
workers' view of, 141–44
Work pace
computerized assembly line and, 112–14, 115
just-in-time production and, 77–78, 114–15

Work rules, 43
Work setting, 62–93
human component, 65–68
plant layout, 63
shop floor reality vs. company philosophy, 85–93
steps in assembling car, 71–76
Body department, 73
Paint department, 73–74
Stamping department, 73
Trim and Final, 74–76
Team 1 tasks, 76–85
typical day, 68–71
Work standards, 10
takt time, 75, 79, 105, 143
Work stations, 64–65, 75
Wrist and hand injuries, 84–93

Yellow cord line stoppages, 78–79, 113

About the Author

Laurie Graham is an assistant professor in the Division of Labor Studies at Indiana University in Kokomo. She received her Ph.D. in sociology from Purdue University.